HOW I LOST
$25,000,000

The Memoir of a Serial Entrepreneur

HOW I LOST
$25,000,000

...Discovered the Secrets
to Business Success,
and Found True Happiness

Ronald Hume

 mosaicPRESS

Library and Archives Canada Cataloguing in Publication

Title: How I lost $25,000,000 : ...discovered the secrets to business success, and found true happiness / Ronald Hume.

Other titles: How I lost twenty-five million dollars

Names: Hume, Ronald, author.

Identifiers: Canadiana (print) 20220169799 |
                Canadiana (ebook) 20220169918 |

ISBN 9781771616362 (softcover) | ISBN 9781771616379 (PDF) | ISBN 9781771616386 (EPUB) | ISBN 9781771616393 (Kindle)

Subjects: LCSH: Hume, Ronald. | LCSH: Businesspeople—Biography. | LCGFT: Autobiographies.

Classification: LCC HC102.5.H86 A3 2022 | DDC 338/.04092—dc23

Published by Mosaic Press, Oakville, Ontario, Canada, 2022.
MOSAIC PRESS, Publishers
www.Mosaic-Press.com
Copyright © Ron Hume 2022

Printed and bound in Canada.

MOSAIC PRESS
1252 Speers Road, Units 1 & 2, Oakville, Ontario, L6L 5N9
(905) 825-2130 • info@mosaic-press.com • www.mosaic-press.com

Praise for How I Lost $25,000,000 ...Discovered the Secrets to Business Success, and Found True Happiness

– – – – – – – – –

"This book is a virtual master-class for entrepreneurs. Readers will learn a strategy to raise capital fast on the best possible terms, how to launch successful sales and marketing programs, recruit the best team, and avoid the potholes that cause many businesses to fail.

I used to think "if only every entrepreneur could have a mentor like Ron" ... and with this book, they now can. Ron Hume has been a source of inspiration and support throughout my own entrepreneurial journey ever since we were introduced during my business school years. He has been who I have turned to for perspective when the lows have been low, and also when the highs have been high. As entrepreneurs we can be myopic in our vision and maniacal in our focus, but that single-minded obsession won't make us happy. Ron gives every reader of this book the gift of perspective. Chosen correctly, the things we do outside of work are not distractions, but the fuel for our ultimate success and happiness, even on the job. Thank you Ron. Let us all take the lessons to heart.

Entien Etuk, Founder & CEO, FitGrid.
Henry Crown Fellow, Aspen Institute.
World Economic Forum Technology Pioneer.
Presidential Leadership Fellow.

"How I lost $25,000,000" captures the roller-coaster ride that is entrepreneurship so well. At a deeper level, the book is a personal reflection on the true nature of success and building a truly good and productive life. There is much to be savoured in Ron's story."

Heather Crosbie, Senior Adviser and mentor to
entrepreneurs at ventureLAB,

Table of Contents

- - - - - - - - -

Introduction: Learn how the mind of an entrepreneur works, and the risks they assume heading off into uncharted waters without a map, operating instructions, or guides to lead the way. Explains the important role entrepreneurs play in a modern economy.

Part 1
In the Beginning

Part 3
The Hume Group of Companies

Part 4
Setbacks and Recovery

Part 5
Valuable life lessons acquired on my journey

The Hume Funds investment managers at a weekly meeting:

The *Hume Group of Mutual Funds* were managed by the high profile investors pictured above. From left to right, Andy Sarlos, Fred McCutcheon, Norman Short, and Dr. Morton Shulman. This photo was taken at a weekly breakfast meeting held in the dining room of Shulman's grand home in Toronto. Ron attended most of these meetings to report on the amount of money flowing into each Hume Fund over the past week and on upcoming marketing initiatives. These were exciting sessions. As money flowing into the funds increased exponentially, the fund managers where challenged on how make stock buys without driving up share prices.

Ron Hume reviewing *The MoneyLetter*:

Ron checking out an early edition of *The MoneyLetter*. This investment advisory was an instant and highly profitable business success. Over 10% of those who enrolled in the Successful Investing and Money Management self-study program subscribed to *The MoneyLetter*. Within six months of being launched, it was one of Canada's top three investment advisory services. A US edition was introduced the following year.

The components in a Hume Publishing self-study course:

All Hume Publishing courses were developed based on sophisticated self-study pedagogical tactics that motivated enrollees to complete the program. Enrollees could request personal counselling when they had problems understanding or applying what they were learning. Exercises and assignments encouraged users to immediately apply what they learned to better manage their personal finances.

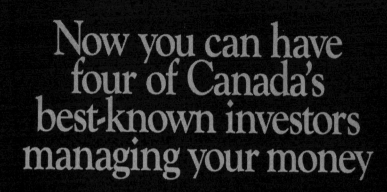

Now you can have four of Canada's best-known investors managing your money

THE HUME GROWTH & INCOME FUNDS

A direct mail promotion for *The Hume Group of Funds*:

Pictured here is a brochure from a direct mail campaign for *The Hume Group of Funds*. These direct mail campaigns were ground breaking in two ways. Hume was the first company to market funds directly to consumers rather than through major financial institutions such as banks, stock brokers, and credit unions. As well, Hume's marketing messages were the first to feature background information on each fund manager.

Hume Publishing's direct to consumer mass marketing programs:

Examples of the highly effective direct mail packages and free standing inserts Hume Publishing used to generate over 250,000 new subscribers per year. Every year over 500,000,000 million direct-sales promotions, similar to those pictured here, were delivered to the homes of consumers in the US and Canada. The response rates for direct mail campaigns averaged about 1.5%.

What is an entrepreneur?

- - - - - - - -

*"You only have to do a few things right in your life
so long as you don't do too many things wrong."*

Warren Buffett

*"Every problem is a gift –
without problems we would not grow."*

Anthony Robbins

*"Business opportunities are like buses,
there's always another one coming."*

Richard Branson

*"Success is not final; failure is not fatal:
it is the courage to continue that counts."*

Winston Churchill

RONALD HUME

"And the day came when the risk to remain tight in the bud was more painful that the risk it took to blossom."

Anais Nin

"There is no shortage of remarkable ideas, what's missing is the will to execute them"

Seth Godin

xiv

Preface

Ron Hume's memoir is a deeply personal story that explores important ideas about business and the entrepreneurial life. He inspires us to follow our dreams and reach for the stars when setting off on a career or founding a business. We learn how it feels to be born with an entrepreneurial gene that enables some to scale the highest peaks in the business world and sustain a meaningful and mindful life, even when confronted with devastating setbacks and hard times.

Ron reveals the details of how he transformed a staid educational and business publishing company into a highly successful best-selling trade publisher; how he developed self-study programs and investment advisory services with over 250,000 annual subscribers; how he broke new ground by founding the first financial services company that sold mutual funds directly to consumers. You will also learn how he survived the loss of his business empire and, despite this monumental setback, turned his life around to find happiness and fulfilment.

This book is a timeless tale that clearly sets out the fine line between success and greed. This story should inspire each of us! Ron reminds us that, in the life of an entrepreneur, it is the chase and the game that adds the spice to life, and drives them on. As well, you will learn timeless life lessons on how to succeed in business in today's faced paced high-tech world, while maintaining a happy and fulfilling personal life.

Even while writing this memoir Ron continues to dream and seek out new business opportunities. He provides incentive to perhaps entice the reader to take on Wall Street, the purest North American gaming house.

Perhaps this memoirs' most important message is to remind us that, in the arc of every life, we must learn how to cope with both great successes and bitter disappointments if we are to achieve true happiness and fulfillment.

This should inspire each of us.

Most of all, me.

Peter Copland

Introduction

- - - - - - - -

I have enjoyed a long and thoroughly delightful career as a serial entrepreneur. Readers of this memoir will learn how the mind of an entrepreneur works, and the risks they are prepared to assume heading off into uncharted waters without a map, operating instructions, or a guide to lead the way.

Entrepreneurs are essential to every society. The businesses they found generate the jobs and pay the taxes that fund our way of life. It is my belief that entrepreneurs are genetically programmed to this way of life. It's not a life that is right for everyone. And that is a good thing as the entrepreneurs who found new businesses are not necessarily best suited to running them on a long-term basis.

For better or for worse, it is clear that I was destined from birth to be an entrepreneur. Since dropping out of high school, I've been a mechanical draftsman, published several award winning books, one of which made it to the #1 spot on the *New York Times* best-seller list, founded a publishing company that became a household name in its niche, developed a self-study program in which over six million people enrolled, and founded a group of mutual funds that were the first in North America to be sold directly to consumers.

Writing this memoir enabled me to see the arc of my life in a new perspective. I've come to appreciate what it takes to live a truly happy and fulfilling life – and it's not having more money. Until my mid-20s, the jobs I worked at were dull and uninspiring. I worked to pay essential living costs, and nothing more. Then, I landed a job in publishing and, from that day until now, I have lived to pursue my passions as a publisher, marketer, and business builder. I've enjoyed an amazing and wonderful ride, running the gamut from thrilling successes to devastating failures. Even now, when most my life-long friends have either retired or expired, I am passionately involved in publishing projects and often wake up bursting with new ideas, and new projects to explore.

This memoir is organized into five sections. The first covers my early years and the struggle to find a fulfilling career; the next, describes how, after getting on the right track, I was able to achieve business success working for a big company. Section three tells the story of leaving the comfort of a corporate job, to become an entrepreneur, and enjoying successes beyond my wildest dreams. Section four tells the story of business reversals, and my struggle to recover and live a happy and fulfilling life. The final section, offers my insights on how to be successful in business and your personal life in order to make the best of every day...until it's time to depart and follow in the footsteps of every person who ever lived.

Entrepreneurs never lose sight of what is most important in life. Making big money and acquiring the most toys does not bring you authentic happiness. Personal fulfillment can only be found by devoting your life to people and projects that interest you, and making the world a better than you found it.

Hope you enjoy the read.

Ron Hume

PART 1

IN THE BEGINNING

Chapter 1

Falling Off a Cliff

‒ ‒ ‒ ‒ ‒ ‒ ‒ ‒

October 19, 1987 was a crisp, clear, autumn day in Toronto. Since mid-morning I'd been holed up with a venture capitalist who'd flown in from New York. Tom was a charming and smooth talking New Yorker who oozed confidence and authority. His perfectly fitting slate grey suit and high-end shoes probably cost almost as much as my car.

I was nervous and felt totally out of my league. I hoped my insecurity didn't show. After a few minutes of small talk about life in Toronto and New York he got right down to business and tabled an offer to acquire the business I'd built over the past 14 years.

Tom's company was part of a syndicate that had developed a keen interest in Hume Publishing and The Hume Groups of Funds. According to their analysis, our organization would be an ideal fit to merge with another business in which they owned the controlling interest. Right up front, he made it clear this was a firm, limited time, and non-negotiable offer.

After all these years, the emotional roller coaster I was riding that day is still vividly clear. Should I try to negotiate a better deal or just accept the deal Tom laid out, and walk off with 25 million for my stake in the company? I'd be lying to say this was not tempting. Maybe I should just tell Tom to sod off. If the syndicate was willing to pay this much, what was The Hume Group really worth? Maybe a lot more than Tom's offer.

It was exciting to think I'd built a business that had attracted the attention of a big league New York venture capital syndicate. Deep down I felt it would be crazy to walk away from a $25,000,000 payout. On the other hand, I was having a lot of fun running the business. At the end of the day, I asked for a week to consider the offer and discuss it with my board and shareholders. He agreed.

I was euphoric when the business day ended. Even if we passed on the offer to sell The Hume Group of Companies, it seemed certain I was going to end up a rich man.

That evening I met my wife Penny for dinner at Orso, one of Toronto's hottest Italian bistros. Penny is smart and beautiful, she loves life in the fast lane. She was over the moon to hear about the day and urged me negotiate a better deal and sell out. After dinner we went on to a performance by the Toronto Symphony orchestra at Roy Thompson Hall. At that moment I was more than a bit pleased with myself. King of my universe.

Taking a seat in the concert hall, Rueben Cohen, President of Central Capital, one of Canada's largest financial institutions, was seated next to me. He was obviously in considerable distress. As a conversation starter, I asked him where the stock market had closed that day. Since the markets were enjoying a record bull run, I expected the thought of another good day on the market might lift Rueben's sullen mood.

As it turned out, my "mood lifting" strategy was a bit off the mark. The market had crashed during the time I was holed up with Tom. The Dow Jones was off on the day by over 20%. The 1987 market crash was underway!

With this news, my exuberant mood vanished. I broke into a cold sweat. One thing was certain – Tom's offer to buy The Hume Group of Companies was gone. And, because our mutual funds company, launched about 18 months earlier, was not yet profitable, I knew my businesses were going to be facing dark and stormy days ahead. This realization hit home, my heart sank.

A morning that began with promise and excitement ended up being one of the darkest days of my life.

Three years later, I had lost control of my businesses, one was bankrupt, Penny and I had parted ways, and I was an emotional wreck.

Despite these monumental reversals, I survived and came to realize that if life didn't have rough patches, it would be impossible to fully appreciate the good times.

My father, who graduated from a technical high school, had an amazing ability to solve highly technical engineering challenges. With these skills, he held down a decent paying job throughout the depression. He always wanted the best for me and my brothers, but lacked the ability to communicate with others, including his family.

My father and I rarely engaged in a meaningful conversation. The day I told him my first marriage was over, his only comment was about the day's weather. Dad was a control freak who would order me about on daily basis. I would get a sharp slap if his orders were not obeyed immediately and flawlessly. This approach to parenting launched me into life entirely devoid of self-confidence and the know-how to work as part of a team.

Mom, however, was warm, loving, and highly intelligent. After raising five sons, and in her early 40s, she went to work for the first time in the steno pool of a major hospital. Within three years she was appointed the personal assistant the Chief of Staff. Mom was generous and warm. She imbued me with the meaning of empathy and its importance in living a truly fulfilling life.

Chapter 2

Early Signs of a Budding Entrepreneur

— — — — — — — —

As high-school days unfolded, so did my awareness of the things that really mattered in life. For instance, while hanging out with my class mates, I began to realize that those who achieved the highest exam marks weren't necessarily the best thinkers in the class. They had an exceptional ability to remember facts, but weren't able to string those facts together and connect the dots when it came to figuring out how best to deal with real life situations. This realization only made me feel worse. Although I felt smarter than most of the top-performing students, my exam grades told a different tale. This didn't seem fair. My insecurity and frustration increased as this reality sank in.

Many years later, during an aptitude test, it was revealed that I suffered from dyslexia. During his first year in school, my son Peter received this same diagnosis. Dyslexia is often an inherited condition that probably affected my Dad too. This likely played a role in my lack of academic achievement.

Before reaching my mid-teens you could not find in me the qualities you would expect to find in a successful entrepreneur.

RONALD HUME

As the years rolled by, it became clear I was never going to achieve great academic or athletic success, or be the life of the party, so I'd have to find other paths to getting ahead in the world.

These thoughts consumed me as a teenager. Eventually, I came to the conclusion that my only path to success was to believe in myself, and my ability to think clearly and logically. I would be prepared to take risks when assessing opportunities. And last but not least, I would never abandon my goals — as long as the facts made it clear I was on the right track. I planned to be ruthlessly persistent in achieving my objectives.

My wife Babs, who I love and adore, says I am the most stubborn man she has ever met. She also claims she has never met anyone so committed to "getting it done now". In other words, I am annoyingly impatient.

Despite a lack of achievement during this early stage of life, I slowly began to acquire confidence by capitalizing on my ability to think logically in identifying opportunities, and being persistent in achieving goals.

This approach to life is shared by many highly successful entrepreneurs. Steve Jobs didn't have a college degree and Bill Gates dropped out of university before getting his degree. Although Elon Musk is a university graduate, he chooses his top aides because of their ability to solve problems rather than their academic achievements.

In the 1950s, teenagers were expected to earn their own spending money. Most of my friends got jobs bagging groceries, working at the local drug store soda fountain, or delivering papers. But an unexpected encounter at the local drugstore, convinced me there was a better way to earn pocket money.

While picking up a prescription for my Mom, I overheard the drugstore owner offering a local sign maker $4 for a sign to post in the store window. At that time, this was big money. The sign was simple in design, and I was confident that I could make equally good ones in about an hour's time. So the next day, I mocked up window and counter display signs and showed them to the drugstore owner, quoting a price of $3 each. He hired me. I was exuberant and ran home to tell my parents that this is how I would earn money.

Although sign making seemed a good way to earn money, assignments were few and far between. I needed a steadier source of income. A few days, later another money making opportunity burst its way into my mind. I was a good snooker player. Although far from a pool shark, I was a consistent winner. So, to supplement my earnings, I would head for pool hall every day after school and take on my school mates, and other kids who spent time there. The stakes were twenty-five to fifty cents a game.

Soon my snooker winnings were bringing in a steady income ranging from $5 to $10 per week. As a bonus, I much enjoyed the guilty pleasure of making money with a pool cue. Because I was somewhat embarrassed by this disreputable means of earning money, I never told my parents, or even my best friends, about my secret life as a pool shark. As it turned out, my skills at snooker were a great cover to justify to my parents how I always had money. By the time I dropped out of high school, I'd never held down a regular part-time job during the school year. But I had accumulated a tidy nest egg of $800.

My first full-time job was working during the summer holidays as a dishwasher at Milford Manor, an up-scale resort in Muskoka. This was dream job for any teenage boy. For the first time in life I was living independently, and, for every guy on the staff, there were three girls who worked as waitresses or cleaning the guest rooms. I was sure to have my first girlfriend by summer's end.

As it turned out my girlfriend quest didn't work out — even at the very favorable three to one odds. My lack of self-confidence held me back from coming on to girls and, when a girl occasionally showed interest in me, I had no clue what to say or do. Happily, as my self-confidence increased over the next few years this serious disability gradually melted away.

Despite the ever frustrating girlfriend issue, I did learn two important life lessons working at Milford Manor. The resort employed a seven piece band that did four gigs a week at the resort's lakeside dance pavilion. And during my second and final summer at the resort, the band leader let it be known they would not be returning the following summer.

As it turned out Jack Giles, one of my classmates at Malvern Collegiate, had a seven piece band that, in my opinion, was every bit as good as the Milford Manor band that needed to be replaced.

As a confirmed dot-connector, I decided that my buddy Jack Giles should have that job. Not surprisingly, Jack was on board with the idea too. But someone had to approach Gordon Reid, the lodge owner, to set up an audition.

Gordy was a huge, gruff, and imposing man. In my mind he was cast from the same mould as my Dad. There was no way he was going to listen to me, a lowly dishwasher, for a recommendation about hiring a band.

I thought about this for several days. My train of thought went like this. I can't contact him personally, I'm too scared and have no credibility. But there is no other option. If I don't do this myself, it will never happen. What have I got to lose by giving it a try? Clearly nothing as I wasn't coming back next summer. What's the worst thing that can happen if I try and fail? Only humiliation, and I'd already lived through this on numerous occasions and survived. What would happen if I tried, and perchance succeeded? I'd be euphoric.

After going through this convoluted thought process, I screwed up my courage, and with my heart thumping like a sledgehammer, knocked on the door of Mr. Reid's home. When he opened the door, I stammered nervously while telling him about the Jack Giles band. He listened politely and asked a few questions. In less than five minutes he had agreed to audition the band when next in Toronto.

The day Jack Giles band landed the Milford manner gig, I was ecstatic! Despite my overwhelming lack of confidence, I had engineered a real deal! As well as being a pool shark, I was a budding creative agent.

Despite the self-confidence issues that had dogged me throughout my years at school, it was also a time when I developed lifelong friendships that have enriched my life beyond measure.

RONALD HUME

I was part of a neighborhood gang of eight that came together when we were in grade school. Over the years we enjoyed a wide range of adventures, and got into some mischief too.

As teenagers, we formed our own hockey team and named ourselves "The Smoothies" and played weekly games against other East End teams at Ted Reeve Arena.

As we had passed through the teen years, a few of the gang members went on to university and others to full-time jobs. At this point we formed an investment club and made a bit of money investing in speculative Canadian mining companies. My stake in these investments was funded through my prowess at the snooker table.

The activities of our core gang continued for another 30 years when we went on annual week-long canoe trips, paddling and portaging though Ontario's Algonquin park during the first week of September. These are glorious memories. There is no better way to establish strong bonds and develop lifelong friendships. On a week-long canoe trip you quickly learn the importance of team work and to accept the strength and weaknesses of your fellow campers. There are few experiences that compare with sharing dinner over a crackling camp fire, then, as dusk turns almost instantly to darkness watching stars fill the sky, listening to pure silence, occasionally broken by the howling of wolves. Then later, nestled into our sleeping bags, we'd discuss the world and plan our future destinies. These were wonderful times.

Two members of this group, Don McGregor and Peter Copland became my best friends. We had this in common.

Each of us were born entrepreneurs who went on to found successful businesses.

Shorter than average with a wiry build, Don was always the life of the party with his acerbic sense of humor. He was a great fan of Frank Sinatra and every time you got into Don's car, the latest Sinatra hit would be blaring at top volume. He was also a highly talented hockey player. Peter is a born leader. Tall and raw boned, Peter has the unmistakable look of an athlete. While attending the University of Toronto he was an all-star linebacker who received, and declined, an offer to play professionally for the Edmonton Eskimos. Peter moved to Victoria where he founded a rowing club and maintained a close relationship with Canada's National and Olympic rowing teams. He continued as a competitive sculler until his mid-70s, reaching the podium in international Master's events about a dozen times, including at least two gold medals. Peter is member of Rowing Canada's Hall of Fame.

Peter was the founder of Chinook Chemicals which eventually, became a leader in it specialized niche. Don founded Permafleur, a company that became Canada's leading distributor of artificial flower and decorative products.

Along the way, each of our companies had their high points and went through rough patches. Whatever the circumstances, we provided each other with unconditional support when one of us got into a jam. For a period of time, when our businesses were at an early stage and growing fast, Peter and I shared the services of a senior level Chief Financial Officer. In the mornings he'd work for Peter and in the afternoons took the subway and spent the afternoon at my office. This worked well for several months until the CFO's mid-day breaks increased to three hours two or three days each week. When confronted with this situation he claimed to be doing missionary work for his church over the mid-day period. Eventually we learned the real truth. He wasn't doing missionary work, he was spending his extended lunch hour in the missionary position with his girlfriend.

Much of my business success can be credited to Don and Peter. Without their enduring support and encouragement, I would never have had the guts, support, and cheerleading required to start my own business. Whenever I needed help, I didn't need to ask for it. Peter and Don were always there to get me through a rough patch.

Sadly, Don passed away when he was seventy, but rarely does a month go by without Peter and me getting in touch. To this day, we both belong the same book club.

Chapter 3

Lost in the Wilderness

– – – – – – – –

Upon leaving school, most of us have two major projects. Find a mate, and establish a successful career. This was not a good time for me. I didn't have a clue what I wanted to be when I grew up. Nor did I have the know-how, experience, or competence with women that's essential to find the right partner and make a happy and fulfilling marriage.

In my small world of middle class East end Toronto, there were few role models for boys other than trades, the police and fire departments, and for those with higher ambitions, perhaps to become an engineer. In my peer group only two of us went on to university, and they each chose engineering.

As far as my father was concerned, mechanical engineering was the only career choice for me. But, since I'd disappointed him by dropping out of high school and had no hope of getting that prized engineering degree, he insisted I enrol in engineering related courses at Ryerson Polytechnic Institute. There was only one problem. I had not the slightest interest in this field of work. But, with my Dad's relentless urging, I enrolled in night courses to qualify as a mechanical draftsman.

During my high school years, I was drawn to the arts. In English we studied Bernard Shaw's *Pygmalion*. I was fascinated by the witty dialogue and twisting plot lines. I couldn't get enough of Shaw at school so I used my pool hall income to buy paperback editions of all Shaw's plays. I read them over and over. We also studied *The Ancient Mariner*, the classic poem by Samuel Coleridge. I fell in love with the wonders of writing techniques such as alliteration, and onimatopia that were used to bring life and vibrancy to lines of text. The day I first heard the clause "the furrow follows free", I felt a thrill course through my body.

Art was another of my passions as a teenager. I spent countless hours drawing. Especially attracted to portraits, I read books on Rembrandt and Michelangelo. I enrolled in a community center evening oil painting course where I was the youngest in the class by about 40 years. I bought a set of artists paint brushes, a pallet, and oil paints. My first paintings were copies of Michelangelo's "Hand of God" from the Sistine Chapel and "Man in the Golden Helmet" by Rembrandt. As I write this book, one of the oil paintings I did that year hangs over the desk in front of me. It's the portrait of a North American Indian.

At the time, with my limited world view and no role models, establishing a career in the arts was never on the radar screen.

Upon completing my course at Ryerson, I landed a junior draftsman's job at Link Belt, the Canadian subsidiary of a

US engineering and heavy equipment manufacturer. What followed was the most boring and dreary five years of my life. We punched a time clock at 8:00 AM each workday. If you were two minutes late, your pay was docked.

About fifty draftsman sat in five rows in one huge room. At the head of each row facing his men, and they were all men, sat the supervisor who doled out our assignments. Most involved the designing of conveyor belts and gear reducers.

Upon receiving an assignment, a draftsman's first job was to do the basic math to ensure the iron and steel specified for the project was sufficiently strong to do the job without breaking down. It was equally imperative you didn't waste money by specifying too much metal. These calculations usually took up about 20% of the time before getting at the job of drawing the plans. As drawings were completed they were sent to "checkers" who reviewed each drawing before the plans were sent to the plant for manufacturing.

For me, this was excruciatingly boring work. I had no passion for designing machines, nor did I enjoy the company of my fellow draftsman. Over lunch and coffee breaks they discussed little other than sports and mundane topics such as how to save money by using powdered rather than whole milk and how to do your own auto body repair jobs. Every day at that job felt like a week. However, because I had some ability as an artist, I was able to turn out neat drawing that attracted the attention of my supervisor.

Then, a couple of years into the job, I read a newspaper article that was to change my life forever. The author had played a major role in designing the Eiffel Tower. It was his contention that when designing a structure, if it looked right, it was almost certainly engineered right. It seemed to me this principle would also be applicable when designing conveyor belts and gear reducers. This was confirmation of something I'd observed in my work at Link Belt. After having completed hundreds of design jobs, I'd come to realize that, without exception, I knew exactly how much metal to specify for a design — without doing the stress and load calculations. So, I decided to stop doing the calculations. What was the point, since every drawing was subject to checking before being released for manufacturing?

With this development, I was able to complete assignments faster than any other draftsman on the floor. My work attracted the attention of the engineer who managed the drafting office. My immediate supervisor told me I was being considered for promotion to a department head. It seems there were three of us competing for this position.

A few days later I was sent to a consulting firm, McQuaid and Ferguson to be evaluated as a candidate for this position. This involved a half-day aptitude test. During the long streetcar ride to the office where the test was being held, I wrestled with a serious question. Did I want to take the test to land the supervisors job, or should I do it to find out what I wanted to be when I finally grew up. It was an easy decision, I wanted nothing more than to get out of the engineering business and find a career that would be interesting.

A week later, I was called back to hear the results from my aptitude tests. As soon as I sat down, the test evaluator told me that, in over a decade of conducting these tests, he had never come across a candidate less qualified for the job. He also said there were a couple of other areas where I had exceptional potential. I was thrilled with this news, and eagerly asked him to tell me more. He chuckled while letting me know this was confidential information that he could not disclose to me because I wasn't paying for the test. I pleaded with him to at least give me a hint. But he was not to be moved.

The next day, I discussed the situation with Gerry, my immediate supervisor. A talented and highly intelligent engineer who had emigrated from the Ukraine, Gerry and I had a good relationship. He'd been advised of my aptitude test results and was pretty sure they'd be part of my personnel file. With some urging, he agreed to visit the personnel department and ask to see my file. It took about a week to get my file and the aptitude study results. At long last, here was the information I'd been seeking since dropping out of high school.

According to the tests, I had an exceptional aptitude for a career in advertising or publishing. With this information, I exploded with joy. The thought of working in these fields had never occurred to me, but as these words issued from Gerry's mouth to my ears, I knew this was the gold at the end of my personal rainbow.

Now my destiny was clear. But this was not to be a fast or easy transition.

Chapter 4

The Clouds Begin to Break

I was now committed to pursuing a career in advertising. At that, time publishing seemed a bit farfetched; however, I could most certainly identify with advertising. But what did I know about the industry? Zilch! So it was off to the library and bookstore to learn how the ad industry worked, and assess job opportunities in this field. I devoured every book I could find on the topic of advertising. With the turning of each page, I knew this was the business for me.

However, before I could focus on finding the perfect job in advertising, Link Belt dealt me one final blow.

When the big cheeses, who headed up Link Belt's engineering team, read the results of my aptitude test, their interest in me plummeted. Then a mining company in Manitoba threatened to sue Link Belt because a conveyor system they'd acquired from the company had iced up during a bitterly cold winter storm. The damage was extensive and expensive. Someone's head had to roll. Turns out, I was responsible for designing this section of the system. As soon as this came to light, I was fired on the spot.

Can't say I was broken hearted but, without a regular pay check, life was going to be challenging until I landed that dream job in advertising. Happily, a freelance drafting job landed in my lap and, because I was still living with my parents, I did not miss any meals.

With the decision made to pursue a career in advertising, I now had to develop a strategy for landing a job in the business.

With no experience or education in advertising, it was clear an illusion had to be created. With a little help from my friends, here is what we came up with.

Gerry, my boss at Link Belt, felt my dismissal was unwarranted so he agreed to provide me with a job reference. I didn't ask him to lie, but all he had to do was tell anyone who called him for a reference that I was smart, energetic, and had worked at Link Belt for four years. My newly created resume was not entirely accurate. It indicated my job at Link Belt was in the advertising department.

My resume now needed to be re-worked to include more evidence of my advertising capabilities. To meet this challenge, my father agreed to give a hand. Over the past couple of years, he had patented an invention for a portable baby highchair. It was very clever. It had the appearance of a neat carrying case. When opened it could be strapped to any standard chair, and one of its sides folded down to act as a tray for the baby.

To pad my new advertising resume, my Dad helped in taking photos of a mom walking along the street with a baby in one arm and a portable highchair held in the other. As well, we did a photo of a baby sitting in the portable highchair and eating. With these photos, I cobbled together a newspaper ad for the portable high chair. The ad never actually ran anywhere, but it did provide substance to my advertising resume.

With my resume completed, it was time to visit the Toronto Reference Library to look for listings of ad agencies and advertising service companies across the country. From these sources, a mailing list was assembled of just under two hundred companies. One of these would surely give me a job upon seeing my newly created resume.

To get out these application letters and resumes was a time consuming exercise. In the 50s, Excel and Window's Word had not been invented. At that time, it was standard practice to send hand written letters accompanied by a typed resume when applying for a job.

Finally, after weeks of finger cramping work hand addressing the envelopes and writing cover letters, my campaign to get a job in advertising was launched.

I couldn't wait for the mail man to arrive as I was expecting job offers. Turns out the campaign was an utter disaster and a monumental waste of time.

Eventually I received two responses. Neither offered a job, but both provided me with a sound bit of advice. When seeking an advertising job, it is best to know how to spell the word "ad". In my portable high chair advertisement I'd used "add" rather than "ad".

Another humiliating experience and an important life lesson: Never send out a mass mailing without first having it copy edited.

This setback did not end my quest to find a job in advertising. It was simply a bump in the road. If nothing else, I had learned how to spell "ad".

The next strategy was to read the classified ad section of all newspapers and trade publications every day looking for available advertising jobs. This meant daily visits to the local news agent to surreptitiously check out, without paying for, the relevant publications. This was a daily task for several months.

Eventually a help wanted ad showed up in the *Toronto Telegram*. McGraw Hill Canada, a publishing company, was seeking a manager for their "promotion department". With my limited industry knowledge it was not clear the position was advertising related, but it seemed close enough. I had nothing to lose by applying for the job, especially since advertising jobs rarely showed up. Moreover, the aptitude test suggested my talents may extend to publishing.

That day my application for the McGraw Hill job went into the mail. I had no expectation of a response. I was seeking an entry level job and McGraw Hill was looking for a manager. But sometimes in life, if you are prepared to take risks, miracles and good things happen. This was one of those occasions.

McGraw Hill's ad was highly misleading as the job they wanted to fill was not a senior position where the successful applicant would be managing a department.

As it turned out, I was the only "junior level" job applicant they received and was invited in for an interview with Barbara Byam who had placed the ad. The interview went reasonably well. She was impressed that I'd worked in the advertising department at Link Belt, and gave the impression I might be considered for the job. Only later did I learn I was the only candidate who would even consider the salary that went with this junior level position. Miss Byam was sufficiently impressed that she asked the company's President, Charles Sweeney, if he'd take a few minutes to see me.

To say I was nervous while being ushered into his office would be a serious understatement. This had to be a joke, me meeting with the President! But we hit it off immediately. In his mid-40s, Sweeney gave the impression of a man in command. He comfortably wore an obviously expensive tweedy brown suit that seemed made for a publisher. With a twinkle in his eye, he came across someone I wanted to know better. After a quick read through my resume, he was impressed that I had worked at an engineering company and asked if I knew how to use a slide rule. After about a half hour of conversation that consisted almost exclusively to him telling me about McGraw Hill, it was clear he liked me, and it was equally clear I was not qualified for the job. But I wanted it desperately!

Without thinking, I blurted out an offer to work free for six months if given a chance to do the job. Mr. Sweeney thought for a minute and said "assuming Miss Byam wants you, I'd consider giving you the job, but there's no way we'd ask you to work for nothing. I'd insist we give you $400 per month for a two month trial period".

At this point, Sweeney called Ms. Byam back to his office, and I was sent to the reception room to await their decision on my future. Five minutes later she returned to announce the job was mine. To say I was ecstatic would be a monumental understatement!

At last, I was emerging from the wilderness — if I could make it through the trial period. And that was certainly no slam dunk.

On the first Monday in August of 1961, I began my career at McGraw Hill Canada. When I walked into those offices as an employee, it was one of my life's most memorable days. The air felt electric and fresh. Everything felt right.

This was big year for me. I was engaged to Patricia, an attractive brunette from Ottawa who came from a large extended Irish Catholic family. Pat was a newly minted nurse who planned to be a "scrub nurse" acting as the principle support to the operating surgeon. We had set a marriage day for October10, just two months after I had joined McGraw Hill.

For the first time in my life, women were playing a major role in my life. Not only was I getting married, I would be working side by side with women. This was exciting, but also a terrifying prospect. On the engineering floor at Link Belt, there was a single female, the big boss's secretary.

My boss Barbara Byam, was in her mid-forties. She was smart, classy, and knew the book publishing business. This was my first experience meeting a women holding a management position. My immediate colleagues were two bright young women who had university degrees. Cathy and Jeanie were both attractive, confident — which I was not — and gave me a warm welcome as their newest team member.

Our Promotion Department was to prepare descriptions of new McGraw Hill books as they were published. These were distributed to the company's sales staff and customers. The books were segregated into four groups: university, elementary & high school, business, bookstores & libraries. As well, we were responsible for putting out two annual catalogues for McGraw Hill's customers in each of these groups.

I was shocked when Barbara Byam informed me that the other team members would be working for me. This was bizarre. I was a high school dropout with no experience in publishing while Cathy had a Master's Degree in English from the University of Toronto and Jeanie had an undergraduate degree in English from the University of British Columbia.

Sadly, this was a typical situation in the 1960s. Neither Cathy nor Jeanie complained about the situation. I wondered how Barbara Byam managed to achieve her status as a manager at the company.

Happily, it is a different world today. Based on my lifetime of experience, it is my belief women are better managers than men. Testosterone charged males are often more inclined to dominate and play politics rather than negotiate and seek the best solutions.

Within a month or so at McGraw Hill it was clear I had managed to find my way through the wilderness, at least on the career side of my life.

PART 2

THE THRILL OF SUCCESS

Chapter 5

A First Triumph

As the months went by at McGraw Hill, my confidence grew, and it seemed the senior management were pleased with the work I was doing. For the first time in my life I could not wait to get to work each day. My colleagues were interesting people. Over lunch we'd discuss, music, theatre, art and politics. This was a breath of fresh air after those dreary days at Link Belt where I shared few interests with my colleagues. There were no time clocks. If you occasionally came to work a few minutes late no one cared, as long as you did your job. At McGraw Hill people really cared about their work. On many occasions our team stayed at the office well in to the evening to finish up projects. This was standard practice at McGraw Hill. You were seldom alone when working late. Other departments shared the same work ethic.

Two months into the job and a month before the trial period ended, my salary was doubled. It still didn't match my Link Belt salary, but I didn't care. For the first time, I was truly enjoying my job.

Six months after starting work at McGraw Hill, my next big break came.

McGraw Hill is one of the world's major business book publishers. In the 60s, pre-Internet, their titles included the standard handbooks used by professionals including engineers, senior management, accountants, economists, etc. Virtually every professional relied on books to stay abreast of new developments in their profession. New titles were published monthly. The updated editions of the major handbooks were a must buy for many professionals. McGraw Hill's catalogue of business publications was over 200 pages long.

Most bookstores did not stock a broad range of business books. They were sold directly to professionals through publishers. McGraw Hill's Direct Mail Department was a powerhouse in this business sector.

Direct Mail was, without a doubt, the least glamorous revenue generating department at McGraw Hill. In Canada, this department mailed out over 10,000 direct mail packages every day of the year. It employed a staff of about 15 – 20, mostly young immigrant women, who printed out addressed envelopes from a wide selection of databases and hand stuffed them with literature describing each new title.

About six months after joining the company, Charles Sweeney, the company's president asked me to take over as Manager of the Direct Mail Department. The department was a consistent money loser and, with a postal strike looming, matters were likely to deteriorate further.

According to Sweeney, this dire situation could only be remedied by bringing in someone who could inject new energy, and a fresh eye, to what had become a chronically money losing department. I suspect the real reason I'd been offered this great opportunity is because no other member of the management team would not touch this "opportunity" with a barge pole.

The position came with a pay raise that I and my new wife welcomed. We could now afford a new car.

Clearly, I could not turn down this promotion. But I was completely unqualified for this position. I knew nothing about direct mail marketing, or how to manage a department of 20 people.

Over the next couple of weeks, including weekends, I arrived home from the office near midnight. I spent my time gathering and pouring over all the available data on the company's direct mail response rates from each mailing list. I looked for seasonal and industry buying patterns, and analysed all department costs. During this period, my slide rule was red hot and I was and dead tired, and I broke out with a stress related skin rash.

After this exercise, I was confident the department could be run at a profit. *But only if big changes could be sold to Sweeney and the Management Committee.*

The numbers revealed that response rates to the company's direct mail campaigns varied greatly depending on the time of the year. The variance between the highest and lowest responding months was over 100%. In the best month, the mailings were generating response rates of more than 2%. That dropped off to less than 1% in the worst performing months of July and December.

The cost analysis suggested we could significantly reduce the costs if the mailings were outsourced to a commercial letter shop. The only issue with out-sourcing was the minimum quantities the letter shops would accept, which was about 100,000 mailings.

Based on this analysis, it seemed probable we could make the Direct Mail Department profitable. At 10,000 mailings per day, this totalled over two million mailings per year. Therefore, we would be highly profitable doing twice yearly mailings of a million, and timing the campaigns for January and September.

This sounded like a reasonable plan. All I had to do now was present and sell it to Sweeney and the company's Executive Committee who met weekly to allocate funding to various publishing projects. This group included the managers of each revenue generating department, with the exception of Direct Mail. It took over a week of working flat out from early morning to late into the evening to complete my report. I was soon to learn how many, otherwise intelligent people, are deathly afraid of change.

When the day came to present my plan I was nervous, worried about embarrassing myself, and felt totally inarticulate. Copies of my Report on the Direct Mail Department had been circulated to the executive committee beforehand. Based on rumors that reached me through my buddies in the Promotion Department, I was warned that my plan was in trouble, even before it was tabled at the meeting.

The meeting was contentious from the outset. The company's CFO was a crusty Brit who liked to throw his weight around and had a reputation of throwing cold water on new ideas. Within a few weeks of my joining the company, he made it clear that, without a university degree, my prospects with the company were extremely limited.

Sitting in front of him when the meeting began was a copy of my report, with the word "Reject" written in bold red letters over the cover page. As the meeting got underway, it seemed clear there were few fans for my proposal in the room that day.

Sweeney kicked off the meeting with a discussion on my proposal for the Direct Mail Department. Immediately, the CFO pompously piped up to offer his obviously negative opinion. Charlie held up his hand to silence the CFO. Then, without further ado announced that he'd read the report in great detail and he loved it. Then he asked who else had studied the plan and, if so, what was their opinion on the report. The room was silent. No one was going to back the CFO when it was clear Charlie had already made up his mind on the issue.

But it did not go all my way at the meeting. Until my theories were proved, Charlie wanted to defer disbanding the in-house crew responsible for getting out the direct mail packages. Instead of sending out an arbitrary total of 10,000 per day, outgoing mail would be accumulated and sent out in batches of 100,000. These were to go out during January, February, and March and over the three month stretch from September to November.

If, after a six month period, this test worked, the company would fully adopt to my business plan. Nobody in the room disagreed with Charlie and, without uttering a single word, my plan was approved. And I was on the hook. If it didn't work, I'd almost surely be looking for a new job.

My first boardroom battle had been won, and I hadn't opened my mouth. During the balance of the meeting each of the department heads made presentations. They were all excellent. Never again would I be intimidated at the prospect of selling my ideas in a board room — as long as a solid case was presented. And I'd learned an important lesson that day. My thinking process was on a par with everyone in that room.

There was another interesting by-product of this meeting. From that day forward, I received automatic invitations to all future management team meetings. The Direct Mail department finally had a seat at the table.

The test was a spectacular success. When the six month revenues came in the average response rates from the direct mail had doubled. For the first time in many years, the Direct Mail department was on track to make a profit.

Charlie Sweeney had bet on me, and his wager had paid off. My stock soared. When New York learned of this Direct Mail Department breakthrough, a reporter was dispatched from the *McGraw Hill News*, a publication that was published monthly and circulated to thousands of employees around the world. I was interviewed by the reporter to learn about my role in turning around a chronically money losing department. This was the front page story in the next issue of *McGaw-Hill News*. For the first time in my life, I was now a star.

Overnight my confidence soared. The world was wonderful and I my shyness was dissolving as if by magic.

Equally important, in Charlie Sweeney, I now had a mentor and champion in high places. I was in awe of Sweeney and watched his every move to learn all I could about business management.

Charlie was a vitally important mentor who inspired me to become a successful publisher. Although it was not required, I made an effort to meet with him for a half hour most weeks to provide updates and get his advice on my department's activities. At these meetings, he would often reveal insights on how to manage a business. Most of what I learned from Sweeney will continue to be applicable as long as humans are managing any kind of enterprise. To this day, I take great pleasure in passing on these insights on to aspiring entrepreneurs and business managers.

Here is the story of how I learned about one of Charlie's most valuable business practices. Every Thursday afternoon, he would shut his office door after returning from lunch. He would never book meetings on these afternoons, not with his management team, and not with outsiders. His secretary was instructed to knock on his door only if world war three had broken out.

No one on the management team knew what was going in Charlie's office on Thursday afternoons, but there was much speculation. The most salacious McGraw Hill employees were convinced he was having it off with one of the company's top educational authors during the afternoons when his office door shut. Others suggested that he was simply taking an afternoon nap.

During one of our weekly meetings, he gave me the real scoop about what he did behind that closed door. Upon learning his secret, I immediately incorporated this into my weekly routine, with one difference. Rather than locking myself up on Thursday afternoon I favor Friday mornings.

Charlie felt that many executives get in trouble because most of their time is spent in meetings and discussing issues, and too little is time is allocated to reflection and analysis. So, one half day each week, he would take the time to carefully review and consider the implications of business related data and intelligence that had crossed his desk during the previous week. He was adamant that important reports and data was not to be simply scanned. To achieve success and avoid disasters, all important data and reports must be digested thoroughly and thoughtfully. My initial report on how to fix the money losing Direct Mail Department was a case in point. The company's CFO had simply skimmed my report on the Direct Mail Department, while Charlie has taken the time to read it carefully checking out the underlying assumptions before jumping to conclusions.

Over the next two years the Direct Mail Department continued to do well, as did McGraw Hill Canada. As well, Charlie Sweeney let me in on another of his innovative business practices. This occurred when he invited the company's entire management team to his cottage on Lake Muskoka for a late autumn weekend. At the time the, only female on the team was Barbara Byam, and she was never invited to these sessions. Eight of us were invited to a weekend of poker, prime barbequed steaks, and an open bar, all at Sweeney's expense. He would arrange for half of us to bed down in the Sweeney family's guest rooms and the others would have beds at a neighbor's cottage. In return, he wanted the gang to bring in his dock for the winter and do some repair work on the road leading into his cottage. These minor tasks would be dealt with on Saturday morning, and then the poker would begin. Charley asked if he could drive to the cottage with me. It was on the trip north that the real reason for these trips was disclosed.

These were dual purpose weekends. He really did need help in getting his wharf out the water before the winter freeze up, but there was another more important reason for these annual getaways. He wanted to vet the junior up and coming management team members to see how they handled a situation when gambling and alcohol were involved.

After receiving a heads up on what was going on, I was a cautious drinker that weekend, and a close observer of how the up and comers on the management team handled themselves. Two of them did not distinguish themselves, and it was clear that Sweeney uncovered a fast but effective means to evaluate the future members of his leadership team.

Chapter 6

Climbing the Management Ladder

━ ━ ━ ━ ━ ━ ━ ━

Then, one fine spring day in 1964, I received another summons from Charlie Sweeney. This time, the department in trouble was responsible for selling to bookstores and libraries. About a year earlier, McGraw Hill had recruited a hot shot sales manager from a major competitor to take over the department and return it to profitability. But the losses continued to mount.

Again Sweeney was looking for someone with fresh eyes to take on this challenge. Again he looked to me to fix a problem. Again, I was terrified.

Where to begin? Obviously step one was finding out what these sales guys were doing now. Next, check all available sales data and learn the different sales patterns for the accounts they sold into. This included public libraries, bookstores and school libraries.

Patricia Clark was assigned to help with this project. A recent graduate from a secretarial course, she was smart, ambitious, with a great smile and charm. She got along with everyone. This turned out to be important asset as we needed customer feedback on their book purchasing protocols. Pat was a master at coaxing our customers to help us gather data and their thoughts on how McGraw Hill could improve its service.

With no experience selling, I arranged to spend a week on the road with one of our most experienced salesmen. His name was Phil. He had been with the company for over ten years and knew everything there was to know about the life of a book salesman. He was a solid performer who followed all of the rules but had no ambitions beyond his current job.

This was a most instructive week. Each salesmen had a territory that included accounts ranging from major bookstores to small village public libraries. On a typical day four to six appointments were booked. The sales volume variance between the biggest and smallest accounts was over 1,000%.

Before arriving in next week's territory sales representatives would call ahead and book appointments. In setting up meetings for the coming week, Phil's list of phone calls was arranged alphabetically. Starting at the top he would work down the list from A to Z.

By the time he got to the last half dozen accounts, his calendar for the week was filled up. When this happened, Phil said "too bad we can't get together this week, but don't worry, I'll catch you next time I'm in town." I asked Phil how often he was unable to arrange a meeting. Turned out this was a common occurrence. In the days allotted to a territory, sales reps expected to miss out on meeting with a few accounts and sometimes those missed were the most important.

Phil explained that it is lonely being on the road for weeks so, in scheduling appointments, most sales reps would first call the accounts with whom they had the friendliest relationships and try to book them in as the last call of the morning or afternoon, followed by lunch, dinner, or drinks. These first booked appointments weren't always with the biggest accounts, instead they went to the best friends. If Phil's behaviour was typical, it was clear these sales representatives weren't aware of the line between business and personal relationships.

It turned out this was not the only, nor the biggest inefficiency, in how the McGraw Hill's book salesmen operated.

During a sales call, which was typically booked for an hour, Phil started off by presenting the hot new novels and general non-fiction titles that were most likely to achieve best seller status. Because most book buyers are also avid book readers, the sales calls would sometimes get off track when the buyer wanted to discuss an upcoming book they found especially interesting. These sidebar discussions sometimes went on for ten minutes or so. As a result, when the meeting came to an end, Phil had not picked up sales on the backlist best-sellers including dictionaries, atlases, books on arts and crafts, classic children's books and novels, etc.

After my week with Phil, it appeared there were a few easy fixes that could jump-start sales to bookstores and libraries.

As it happened, a salesman who covered Western Ontario had recently resigned and had not yet been replaced. So I arranged to take this territory over for a month in order to test my newly developed theories on how to increase sales to bookstores and libraries.

In setting up each week's sales meetings, I first called the biggest accounts in the territory. When these appointments were nailed down. This left room for only a few small bookstores. This resolved the issue of missing major account sales calls.

Now, I wanted to test a theory on how to increase the average revenue per sales call by changing the selling sequence. Rather than starting each sales meeting by presenting new titles, the first item on my agenda was to first pick up orders on basic backlist books. The new books and potential best-sellers were left to the end of the meeting. I was confident no bookseller would shut down a meeting before hearing about the hottest new titles.

In making my first solo call as a salesman, it turned out my teenage insecurities were still well entrenched. Before getting up the nerve to meet with my first book buyer I walked around the block a couple of times.

At month end when the sales results were tallied, there was reason to believe my bookselling theories might be effective. Sales in the test territory I was selling into were up 15% over the previous year. Sales were flat in territories where agents continued using their usual sales tactics. This increase in sales was more than expected. I was determined to test these book selling tactics on a broader scale. But knowing how to increase sales was the easy part. Being able to implement these changes was not so easy.

William, the sales manager at the time, resented me being parachuted in to help him increase sales. He was understandably resentful. Particularly so since I had no experience in selling anything including books, nor had I any sales management experience.

A man in his fifties, William had spent a quarter century working his way up to the point where he was the sales manager. He was a tall, charming, good looking man who felt my theories on selling books were naive and unworkable. As well, he had been around long enough to understand how office politics work.

He perceived me as a threat. To protect his turf, William approached members of the management committee where he was well liked. His objective was to have me dispatched back to the Direct Mail Department. This was my first experience with company politics. It was not pleasant. Sweeney summoned me to his office. He asked my level of confidence in the sales tactics I was advocating. My response was yes, 100%.

His responded, "OK, you have my support. You were sent in to fix a problem, and if William won't work with you, he'll have to be fired. And you must do it today. This cannot be allowed to fester and upset the rest of the sales team."

My jaw dropped. It never occurred to me that I had the authority to fire William. I was just a carpetbagger sent in to help him fix a problem. When I explained this to Sweeney, he said, "Well, I'm telling you now, you do have the authority to let him go." And when William is gone, I want you to take over as Sales Manager... as well as your job running the Direct Mail Department."

I had never fired anyone. I broke into a cold sweat. William was well liked, and I was not keen at the prospects of turning a colleague into an enemy. As well, I was concerned how this would go over with the other salesmen. Would they respect me after I fired William?

Sweeney showed me no mercy and made it clear that handling dismissals was just part of every management job. He did relent somewhat. It was a Tuesday and I was given until Friday to let William go. The rest of the week was hell. After missing a night's sleep, I realized it would have been better had William had been fired on Tuesday as Sweeney had suggested.

In the end, there was no problem with the salesmen. They knew the department was in trouble and were relieved to see the back of William. Although everyone in the department liked him, they were aware that the department was going nowhere under his management.

It's a different world today. Now, with client relationship software (CRMs), it's easy to manage and organize all sales and activities, from face-to-face meetings to fully automated digital follow-up processes. This is, without a doubt, powerful software that has revolutionized the field of sales and sales management.

However, sometimes human nature has the ability to over-ride even the most powerful software. Over the past year, I've experienced this reality first-hand. A top-producing sales engineer who regularly exceeds his annual sales budgets confessed to me that, when visiting Toronto, he always sets up his meetings with friends in the city – before reaching out to prospective new clients.

On learning this, I was taken aback. He responded that he knew this was costing him sales, but since he was already ahead of budget for the year, he was not concerned. I wondered if his immediate supervisor felt the same way.

The opportunity to turn around under-performing departments presented to me by McGraw Hill played a vital role in enabling me to become a successful entrepreneur. Both the Direct Mail and the Sales Management departments were consistently underperforming before I was given the opportunity to turn them around. When taking over these departments, previous managers were reluctant to make major changes. Instead, they tried to improve profitability by making minor changes to basically flawed operating systems. My approach was to tear down the broken systems and rebuild them from the ground up based on research.

Without the confidence established by successfully rejuvenating McGraw-Hill's Direct Mail and Trade Book Sales departments I would never have had the confidence to strike out on my own and found Hume Publishing.

Chapter 7

An Introduction to Publishing

— — — — — — — —

Shortly after adding the Trade Book Sales Department to my portfolio, Charlie Sweeney was promoted to Senior Vice-president of McGraw Hill International and moved to New York. I was sorry to see him leave Canada. He was replaced by John McMillan the Vice-President in charge of the company's College Division. John was a gentle man. He had steadily worked his way up the ladder by doing everything by the book without upsetting any apple carts. He was a stark contrast to Sweeney who was innovative, ambitious, and clever. As part of a management change when Sweeney departed, I would now be reporting to Lorne Wilkinson who became the company's Executive Vice-President. Lorne was a tall charming man who was competent and well liked, but not particularly innovative. We got along well, and I made sure we met regularly to keep Lorne in the loop with my trade book publishing plans. He was excited at the prospect of McGraw Hill Canada becoming major player in the Canadian trade book publishing sector.

With my mentor out of the picture, I was now in charge of my own success at McGraw Hill. The opportunity that attracted me was to become a successful trade book publisher. The term "trade books" may sound as dull as dishwater but it's the most exciting field of publishing. As a trade book publisher your job involved working with, and cultivating, best-selling fiction and nonfiction writers. These are interesting, highly creative people with innovative ideas.

At that time McGraw Hill Canada published books almost exclusively for Canadian educational markets. Occasionally a trade book would be published, but these were few and far between. At that time the company had no organized trade book publishing program.

It was my ambition to publish a steady stream of best sellers. The first step in the process was to determine what kind of books had the greatest likelihood of achieving best-seller status. The options are infinite: fiction or non-fiction was the first decision to make. By this time, I was aware that best-selling fiction seldom comes from new authors. The Greshams and Updikes of the world didn't attain their best-selling author status overnight. They had to be carefully nurtured by skilled editors over many years. When I assumed responsibility for McGraw Hill Canada's trade publishing program, we had no editorial capacity to publish fiction.

Non-fiction is a different story. With a hot topic, great title, and celebrity author, there is a long history of instant best-sellers. It was an easy decision to follow this route. To determine the non-fiction topics that most frequently became best sellers we obtained five years of back issues of the *Publisher's Weekly* and *New York Times* best seller lists. This easy-to-do research revealed that cookbooks, weight loss, and books on money management and how to get rich, regularly topped the charts.

Publishing a book on how to get rich was my first choice. Not everyone wants to cook or lose weight, but pretty much everyone in my circle is attracted to the thought of getting rich.

It seemed to me we would have a good shot at publishing a best-seller by finding someone who held down a regular job and — on the side — had become rich by figuring out how to make shrewd investments. It was important our author did not work for a stock broker or financial institution.

Now, the challenge was finding our author. If we could come up with a high profile celebrity who had become rich through his/her own efforts, we could arrange to have the manuscript ghost-written by an established financial journalist,

As you've discovered by reaching this point in the book, I am a lucky guy who regularly crosses paths with interesting opportunities that appear out of the blue. And this happened when setting out to find that "easy way to riches" author.

Within a week, one of Toronto's daily newspapers ran a front page story with the headline "*Shulman Raps Phony Stock Deal*". The moment this somewhat obscure headline caught my eye, I felt we may have found our first bestselling author. Here's why.

At that time Morton Shulman had gained celebrity status in Toronto. He was the city's Chief Coroner, on a mission to save lives. He was relentless in perusing politicians and bureaucrats to reduce unnecessary deaths cause through poor highway design, medical malpractice, inadequate construction safety measures, and the sale of quack medicines. As Chief Coroner he saw his responsibility to act as a public safety watchdog.

Shulman was also a master publicist. He'd hold press conferences where people whose lives had been ruined in accidents that should have been prevented were interviewed. He railed against government incompetence. The press ate this up and so did the public. Anything Shulman did was front page news.

Through the article in the *Globe and Mail*, it came to light that Shulman was also a part-time investor who'd become rich by sussing out shrewd investment tactics unknown to the general public.

Here was the ideal author to write a best-selling book on how to get rich.

The next day, I called the office from where Shulman conducted his practice as a family doctor. Ann, his secretary answered the phone, and I asked for an appointment to see if the good doctor might be interested in writing a book. I could hear her calling out "Morty, I've got some guy on the phone who wants you to write a book, do you wanna see him?" I had an appointment with Morty the following afternoon.

When this development was reported to my boss Lorne Wilkinson, he asked to join me at the meeting. It lasted all of twenty minutes. Yes, Dr. Shulman would be interested in writing a book on how to get rich. But he wasn't doing it on spec. He wanted an advance against royalties of $10,000. At the time this was a monumental advance for a first time author. He said "come back with a contract, and a check for $10,000, and we have a deal. And there's one more condition you'll have to write into that contract. I want to be paid royalties every second month."

Lorne and I rushed back to the office hyped at the prospect of McGraw Hill Canada landing a celebrity author. We immediately barged into John Macmillan's office. A very cautious man, he nearly fell out of his chair at the prospect of giving a $10,000 advance to a first time author. Paying out royalties every two months was out of the question, it had never been done before.

John asked Graham England, the company's CFO, into his office and for the next two hours the four of us discussed and argued over Shulman's demands. Surprisingly, the usually ultra conservative CFO opined that it was really not a problem to pay bi-monthly royalties. In the end, Macmillan gave his reluctant OK to the deal, and it was agreed I could present a contact to Shulman the following day.

Shulman was in the examination room with a patient when I walked into his office. His secretary called through to let him know I'd arrived. Within seconds he appeared at the examination room door and motioned to me saying "come on in, I'm sure Mrs. M won't mind." Mrs. M almost certainly wasn't entirely comfortable with the situation, but in I went. Mrs. M was covered and lying on the exam table. Shulman held out his hand for the contract, and while we stood side by side over Mrs. M, he read through it and said "looks OK to me, where's my $10,000?" He signed the contract asked Mrs. M to witness it. I handed him the advance check then he called Ann into the exam room, handed her the contract and check while asking if she'd transcribe the manuscript. In return, Morty offered to pay her 10% of his royalties.

Within less than a half hour, I was driving back to the office with a signed contact, as happy as a newly minted publisher could be.

It was a good day too for Ann, Shulman's secretary. She'd just agreed to take on a typing job that would eventually earn her over $200,000.

All in all, this was decent day's work for all of us.

For the next 25 years, Shulman would play a pivotal role in my life. He was a handsome wiry man who exuded energy. He was an ardent collector of art and antiquities. In the hallway of his home hung two small elegant Renoir portraits. For a time, he owned the largest private collection of Kreighoffs. His most fascinating collection was one of the world' biggest collections of pornographic clocks and watches. Many of these had been acquired from Egypt's deposed King Farouk.

Highly intelligent, Shulman was a master bridge player and investor. As an investor he prided himself in finding ways to legally game the system. For instance, when he learned a company was going to be acquired or have its shares bought back, Shulman would buy a few shares in the company and then refuse to participate in the share buy back until being paid a huge premium. Shulman eventually founded a pharmaceutical company and promoted its shares to everyone he knew, including me. One day he called with the news that all the shares in his IPO were committed, but he'd set aside a small allotment for me. They were mine if I'd send him $14,000 the next day. As it later came to light, I was one of the first, not the last to be offered shares. However, this this worked out well. Less than two years later he bought back the shares for $200,000.

Within four months of signing his contact with McGraw Hill, Shulman had set two records in the Canadian trade publishing industry. He had received the biggest advance ever, and wrote the complete manuscript for a 250 page book in less than 90 days.

As soon as his book contract was signed, Shulman would sit down at his dining room table after dinner each evening and didn't get up until he'd written a complete chapter of the book. This was after spending a full day seeing patients and carrying out his duties as Ontario's Chief Coroner.

What's even more remarkable, he wrote the entire manuscript by hand using a ball point pen. When the manuscript was completed the book was assigned to Marnie Collins, one of our brightest and best young editors. Marnie suggested we refer to the book as *Anyone Can Make a Million* as a working title until we came up with something better. In the end no one could come up with something better.

Morty had another trait — he was an unapologetic womanizer. During the initial meeting between Morty, me and Marnie, the very attractive editor who'd been assigned to the book, he asked, "when do I get to go to bed with my editor?" Quick witted Marnie, shot back, "I'm yours when your book sells over 100,000 hard cover copies." At the time, no Canadian trade book had come close to this mark. But Morty had an excellent memory and this bet would soon back to haunt Marnie, and cause me some angst too.

About two years later, when word came through from New York that *Anyone Can Make a Million* had achieved best seller status and sales had broken through 100,000. I immediately called Morty to report the good news.

That evening at close to midnight I was in bed with my wife when our phone rang. Calls at this late hour aren't usually to report good news, and this call was no exception. Marnie was on the phone shrieking that I had to get down to her apartment immediately. Shulman was banging on her door, demanding she pay off on their bet. Marnie's neighbors were threatening to call the cops.

To stop the police from coming, Marnie eventually let Morty into her apartment telling him I was on my way to join them. It took over an hour to convince Morty he should go home to his wife's bed.

Anyone Can Make a Million was an amazing publishing story. Because of its intriguing title, coupled with Morty's celebrity and penchant for publicity, the book quickly shot to number one on Canadian best seller lists.

Based on the books remarkable sales in Canada, I phoned the head of McGraw Hill New York's trade publishing division and pitched him on doing a US edition. His immediate reaction was decidedly negative, claiming the content was too Canadian and no one in the US would be interested in buying a book on investing written by an unknown Canadian doctor.

But I wasn't prepared to take no for an answer. When it became clear phone calls would never convince this guy to do a US edition, I decided to develop a US ally to help in getting a US version of *Anyone Can Make a Million* published. I booked a meeting with McGraw Hill New York's head of trade book publicity. Before heading to New York a report on Shulman was put together highlighting his extraordinary ability to generate publicity. With this, and a report on the skyrocketing Canadian sales, my trip to New York was booked.

Not surprisingly, after seeing the backgrounder on Shulman, the New York publicist realized Morty would be a dream author to work with. Over lunch we discussed Morty, and by the time coffee was served she was solidly onside to pitch the trade book editor on a US edition of *Anyone Can Make a Million*.

The next step was arranging a meeting between the trade book editor-in-chief, the publicist, and me. Although not convinced that a US edition of *Anyone Can Make a Million* would even break even, the Editor-in-Chief reluctantly agreed to print 3,500 copies and give it a try.

Now, enthused about the book's prospects, the publicist arranged to have Shulman as a guest on New York's "Long John Nebel" radio shows that aired from 11:30 PM to 5:00 AM.

This show did not have particularly large audience; however it turned out that Johnny Carson was one of the few who tuned into the "Long John Nebel" show that fateful night.

The following day, Carson's people got in touch with McGraw Hill's publicity department and Shulman was booked for an appearance on the "Johnny Carson show". He insisted I accompany him on the flight to New York. It was a bumpy flight and Shulman spent much of it clutching my arm. Although jumpy in a plane Morty wasn't the bit nervous at the prospect of appearing on America's number one late night show. While I sat in the green room watching a monitor and being nervous, Morty was a smash hit during his first appearance on the Johnny Carson show.

With this success, the publicity opportunities for Morty came fast and furious. These included the Merv Griffin show and several follow-up guest appearances with Johnny Carson.

Books began flying out of the bookstores. The, as yet unconvinced, New York editor-in-chief ordered two more small printing of 3,500 before accepting he was dealing with a best seller and arranged a printing of 50,000. Eventually over 2,000,000 copies were printed in the US and Canada.

By July 1967, *Anyone Can Make a Million* was the number #1 non-fiction best seller in the United States.

As a result, my career at McGraw Hill Canada also soared.

1967 was Canada's centennial celebration and the world flocked to celebrate the occasion at Montreal's Expo 67. My best friend Peter Copland suggested he and wife Chris together with my wife Pat spend a week in July visiting Montreal to take in Expo 67. Because the hotels were fully booked during all of that summer, Peter came up with a brilliant alternative. He arranged for us to rent a 50 foot yacht moored at the Expo 67 marina. The deal was, we'd live on the boat, but it must stay moored. It was a perfect solution.

By mid-week we decided to take a one day break from Expo 67 and visit downtown Montreal. As soon as we arrived in the city, I picked up a copy of the *Globe and Mail*. Before leaving on our holiday, my boss Lorne Wilkinson gave me the heads up that I'd been recommended for a promotion, and when it was approved, there would be an announcement in the *Globe and Mail*. There was no expectation the announcement would appear before the following week. But, just in case, I picked up a copy of the paper. Opening it to the business section, there was the announcement of my appointment to Group Vice-President at McGraw Hill. This was a special occasion and we decided buy a bottle of Champagne to enjoy with dinner on the yacht that evening.

After enjoying a wonderful French lunch in Montreal's Old Towne, we headed for Ogilvie's, Montreal's finest department store. While Pat and Chris went off on their own to do some shopping, Peter and I decided to visit the book department to pick some reading for rest the week.

Upon entering the book department, we saw a large display table at the center of the room stacked with copies of *Anyone Can Make a Million*. Over the table were huge 2' x 3' blow-ups of the best seller lists from The *New York Times* and *Publisher's Weekly*. Circled in red on both lists at the #1 position was *Anyone Can Make a Million*.

After the days my children Charron and Peter were born, that Thursday in Montreal was the happiest day of my life!

Chapter 8

The Best Job in the World

- - - - - - - - -

The next few years were a hoot. There cannot be a more inter-esting and stimulating job than being a trade book publisher. The key to success is finding and signing up authors who have something to say, the ability to write, and the celebrity status to sell books. Over the next three years my days were spent lunching or meeting over drinks with celebrities from every walk of life. These prospective authors ranged from the Angli-can Bishop of the North, Jacque Plante the all-star goalie for the Montreal Canadiens, Lister Sinclair the highly acclaimed broadcaster and science writer, world famous artists includ-ing A. J. Casson and Alex Colville, broadcasters including Patrick Watson of *This Hour has Seven Days* and Max Fer-guson CBC's famous morning show host, family court judge Bill Little, Don Harron the great Canadian humorist, and the acclaimed cartoonist Doug Wright.

Not all of these prospects were signed up to write books for McGraw Hill. But wooing prospective authors over lunches at Toronto's finest restaurants and late afternoon drinks the roof-top floor bar of The Park Plaza hotel had to be one of the world's most enjoyable jobs. Particularly so when compared to those dreary and dreadful years I spent as a draftsman with Link Belt.

Some of the successful books we published during this period included Max Ferguson's *And Now Here's Max*. This was a best-seller that won the Stephen Leacock Award for Humor, a successful biography of John Diefenbaker by Tom Van Dusen, Don Herron's *Charlie Farquharson's Hisrty of Canada* and several hockey books including biographies of the Toronto Maple Leaf's King Clancy and Jacques Plante, the famed goalie for the Montreal Canadians who was the first goalie to use a face mask. More than just a hockey player, Plante was an accomplished knitter. One of my favorite books published during this period was *The Tom Thomson Mystery* by Bill Little.

McGraw Hill's list of trade books exploded in 1970 with the acquisition of The Ryerson Press. This turned out to be another interesting opportunity for me. At the time, Ryerson had thousands of titles, most of which were selling fewer than 100 copies a year, and many of the cover designs were outdated. I was assigned the job of culling the list of titles that were no longer profitable, and to manage the redesign of out-date cover art on the best-selling books. This was a monumental task that took over a year to complete. By the end of this process, McGraw Hill had dropped over 25% of the titles acquired from Ryerson. This culling and the redesign of the better-selling titles was a highly profitable exercise. With re-designed covers, sales of most titles increased dramatically. One of these was *Anne of Green Gables* by Lucy Maud

Montgomery where sales increased by over 25% in the year following the re-design of the cover.

Through the acquisition of Ryerson, McGraw Hill had a backlist of trade books from established authors including E.J. Pratt, Dorothy Livesay, Earl Birney and Hugh Hood. As well, we picked up the rights to Alice Munroe's *Lives of Girls and Women*. One of Canada's most distinguished writers, Alice went on to win numerous literary awards including two Giller Prizes and The Nobel Prize for Literature in 2013. After this acquisition, McGraw Hill's Ryerson was a major player in Canadian trade book publishing.

To generate publicity when launching an important new trade book, we would organize a launch party at some interesting venue. Invitations would go out to the press and celebrities in order to generate pre-publication buzz.

For the launch of Morty Shulman's *Anyone Can Make a Million*, we held the launch party at the Sutton Place in their Club 33 room overlooking downtown Toronto. Because of Morty's celebrity status we had more gate crashers than invited guests. There was also the issue of how to throw out an unruly group of pot smokers without disrupting the party.

One of the most successful parties was held on Captain John's ship restaurant moored in Toronto Harbour. This was to launch two works of fiction; *Alice Munro's Lives of Girls and Women* and *Hugh Garner's Cabbagetown*. When these books were published, Alice Munro was at the early stage of a brilliant career as one of the world's most acclaimed writers. Garner was at the other end of the spectrum. For decades

Garner was a renowned Canadian author and *Cabbagetown* was to be his last novel.

The day following this launch party, both Munro and Garner were booked to set off on national publicity tours. Our publicist had arranged pre-scheduled interviews with media in major markets across Canada. Sadly, Garner who was a recovering alcoholic, fell off the wagon at the launch party and disappeared for several weeks missing the entire publicity tour.

My favorite launch party was for Bill Little's book *The Tom Thompson Mystery*. This was held at Ontario's McMichael Gallery of Canadian Art. Boasting the world's largest collection by Canada's acclaimed Group of Seven, this spectacular gallery of log cabin design, is located near the village of Kleinberg about twenty miles north of Toronto to blend in with the surrounding woodlands. At this launch party, I had the pleasure of meeting and discussing the Group of Seven's art with the gallery founders, Signe and Robert McMichael.

One of the most financially successful books we published during this period was *The Money Book: your complete guide to successful money managing and investing* authored by Bill Reddin, a professor at the University of New Brunswick. Originally published as a text book by McGraw Hill, Canada's el-high division, it seemed to me this book might be of interest to a broader audience if redesigned to remove student exercises, and with a new cover that didn't have the look and feel of a textbook. When they heard my plans for marketing the book, both the author and manager of the el-high division were quick to agree.

As soon as the trade edition of The *Money Book* was published, we reached out to the manager of The Hudson Bay Company's book department with a proposal. As one of Canada's biggest department stores, they mailed hundreds of thousands of invoices each month to their customers who bought on credit.

My idea was to insert a stand-alone sales flyer promoting *The Money Book* along with each monthly invoice. The Bay agreed to this arrangement, and we provided the printed sales stuffers free of charge. Through this promotion, we sold over 20,000 copies of *The Money Book*. At that time even best-selling Canadian trade books didn't sell at this rate.

Although I didn't know it at the time, within the next three years, marketing success of *The Money Book* was to have a profound impact on my career.

One of the most unnerving situations encountered during my career as a trade book publisher occurred just after Aleksandr Solzhenitsyn's manuscript for *The Gulag Archipelago* was leaked to the west. Every major publisher was now on the lookout for the next book to be smuggled out from the USSR revealing further Soviet outrages and atrocities.

At the height of this excitement, a telephone call came to my office from the board member of a Toronto-based Ukrainian social club. He wanted us to know that a highly sensitive manuscript was being smuggled out of Ukraine and would be delivered to a member of his social club the next day. The author was a leading dissident currently languishing in a Ukrainian labor camp. After checking out the caller, it turned out he had a sterling reputation in the business community.

This call had to be taken seriously. Clearly this was a book that should be published out of New York.

A call was immediately set up with the editor-in-chief of McGraw Hill's Trade Publishing Division in New York. Upon hearing the story he was excited and offered to fly to Toronto the next day. A meeting was arranged at the Ukrainian social club where we were joined by my New York colleague. We met with the board member who had called me and his friend who had the manuscript. Because the manuscript was written in Ukrainian, they read us portions in English. Based on what we heard, the New York editor-in-chief was excited. But, before agreeing to publish the book, he first had to have the manuscript read and reviewed by a Ukrainian speaking professor in New York who could determine its credibility and worthiness. It was agreed McGraw Hill could have the manuscript to review for a week. Because the Ukrainian social club didn't have a copier, we could take the manuscript with us that afternoon as long as we'd agree to have it copied with the original returned to the club the following day.

We shook hands. My New York colleague picked up the bulging brown envelope containing the manuscript and we departed. By now it was nearing dinner time. He suggested we have dinner together at his hotel. Then I'd take the manuscript to my office to be copied in the morning. The editor-in-chief would come by the office, pick up his copy, and he would deliver the original manuscript to the social club on his way to the airport.

Sounded like a good plan. We hopped into a cab and headed for the hotel. After a superb steak dinner, a fine bottle of Shiraz, and an after-dinner glass of port, we were feeling pretty good. Over the past 48 hours, we had landed what could be blockbuster book. But the day went from great to disastrous when my New York colleague suddenly realized he'd left the manuscript in the cab.

What followed were a series of frantic phone calls trying to locate the cabbie we'd ridden with. This was before everyone carried a mobile. It took until dawn to find the manuscript. During those unnerving seven hours, I worried that this was the end of my career in publishing.

The moral of this story is self-evident.

As it turned out, the New York professor who reviewed the manuscript felt it wasn't sufficiently compelling. McGraw declined to publish. In the business of trade publishing you have to be prepared to kiss many frogs before coming up with the few books that turn out to be best-selling princesses.

Chapter 9

A Life Changing Event

- - - - - - - -

My life as a happy trade publisher was threatened in 1970 when McGraw Hill New York acquired two Washington-based home study companies: Capital Radio and Engineering Institute and Capital Radio Institute. When acquired, neither of these companies were doing business in Canada.

Harold McGraw, the company's CEO saw this as an outstanding opportunity for his thriving Canadian subsidiary. With this announcement, the President of McGraw Hill Canada called a meeting of the company's Executive Committee. There was a single item on the agenda. Who amongst us would assume responsibility for developing a McGraw Hill's "home study" division in Canada? Everyone at the meeting, including me, was appalled at the thought of getting involved in "home study". This was beneath the dignity of our company and our management group. With no volunteers to take on the home study division, John Macmillan who was chairing the meeting pointed his finger at me and said, "then I'm volunteering Ron".

This was not what I wanted to hear.

The next day, arrangements were made for me to fly to Washington and spend a week learning about the home study business. As it turned out, McGraw Hill's newly acquired home study companies were holding a joint sales meeting that week in New Jersey. By attend these sales meetings I would have a great opportunity to meet the senior management team of McGraw Hill's newly minted home study division. Sitting in on these sales training sessions would give me a great way to learn the business.

Upon arriving at the sales conference, I was shocked to find I'd been seated beside Curtis Benjamin, McGraw Hill's' Chairman of the board and the President, Harold McGraw. It would be an understatement to suggest I was nervous.

As it turn out Benjamin and McGraw were in for a shocking morning too.

After opening remarks, the first item on the sales meeting agenda were presentations from top-producing sales reps from each of Capital Radio and Engineering Institute and Capital Radio Institute. Each of these men had a fifteen minute segment to pass on their successful sales techniques.

Most of those enrolling in McGraw Hill's newly acquired home study programs were recently discharged from the military and eligible for tuition support if they enrolled in certified courses, including those offered by Capital Radio and Engineering Institute and Capital Radio Institute.

The first presenter worked the Norfolk Naval base in New Jersey. His secret to success was setting up arrangements with petty officers assigned to aircraft carriers, submarines, and other big warships. They acted as his sub-sales agents.

Petty officers knew the sailors who were due to leave the service and would be eligible for government tuition support.

These sub-sales agents were offered a cash bonus for each sailor who signed up for a Qualified Course using a registration form co-signed by the co-operating petty officers. The sailors were also offered a bonus. By signing up for a course before disembarking, they got a free pass to a local brothel. For young men who had been away at sea for several weeks or months, this was a powerful motivator to seeking higher education. At the time, women were excluded from serving at sea alongside men.

On hearing this story Curtis Benjamin and Harold McGraw went ballistic. Heads were going to roll. Because they were sitting beside me, I knew who was headed for door. Among them was the man I was scheduled to meet with me the next day.

This episode was to change my life forever. My reason for visiting Washington was to learn how to sell home study courses. But when the guy who was to provide this training was fired I was foisted off to the executive in charge of home study course development. Although I cannot remember his name, he provided an impressive introduction to the field of home study, sometimes referred to as "self-study". This was a highly developed method of teaching and he provided the stats to prove its effectiveness.

During subsequent meetings, I did learn how the McGraw Hill self-study programs were marketed in the US, which was largely dependent on selling courses subsidized by the Department of Defence. However, this situation was not applicable in Canada. In my view, if we were to be successful in selling McGraw Hill's home study courses in Canada, we'd need a new strategy.

At this point, dots began to connect in my mind.

Dot 1: Based on our successes with *The Money Book* and Morty Shulman's *Anyone Can Make a Million*, it is clear there is a large market for know-how on how to manage money and become a successful investor.

Dot 2: There were few, if any, courses the average person can take to acquire this highly sought after know-how.

Dot 3: During my time in Washington, I'd been given a primer on how to develop effective self-study programs.

Dot 4: In setting up McGraw Hill's direct mail operations, I'd learned how to market intellectual products directly to consumers.

As these four dots connected in my mind, an alarm bell began ringing at fever pitch.

McGraw Hill should develop a home study on the topic of successful investing and money management. This would be marketed direct to consumers using the company's well-established direct mail operations.

Over the following week, I developed the curriculum for a proposed home study course in successful investing and money management. This was based on the content of *The Money Book* and *Anyone Can Make a Million*.

This was pitched to my boss Lorne Wilkinson and John Macmillan, the President of McGraw Hill Canada.

In no uncertain terms, I was directed to do what I'd been tasked to do: sell the current Capital Radio and Engineering Institute and Capital Radio Institute courses in Canada.

This was an order. John Macmillan said "We haven't sold a single home study course in Canada, and already you're suggesting we spend over $100,000 to develop a new course from scratch. This is crazy".

But I believed in the idea, passionately! So, I asked permission to pitch it to the newly appointed head of McGraw Hill's Distance Education Division in Washington. John and Lorne gave me the go-ahead and a meeting was set up for the following week. It went badly. There was no interest in Washington for developing self-study programs for the consumer market.

For the first time in my short publishing career, McGraw Hill would not support a publishing project I believed in.

I discussed these frustrations with my friend Peter Copland. His opinion meant a lot to me. After completing an MBA degree, Peter had founded Chinook Chemicals when he became frustrated working with big companies including Dow Chemicals. His advice was to set my own company to develop and market the Successful Investing and Money Management home study program.

This seemed like a pipe dream. After working at McGraw Hill Canada for ten years, I was now a group vice-president and making a great salary. Leaving all this behind to start my own business seemed the definition of insanity, especially with two young children and monthly mortgage payments on a new home.

But once implanted, it was impossible to dislodge the dream of having my own business. For months these thought fermented in my brain.

During this period the culture at McGraw Hill changed. I was now at a level in the company were politics was blatant. Until becoming a group vice-president, I'd been relatively immune from company politics. Other members of the executive team considered me outside of the mainstream of the company's business. I was not considered a threat in competitions for the top level jobs.

At that time, there was a retirement coming up that would open up a big job. Although I didn't consider myself a candidate for this position, others at my level did. The politics and dirty tricks involved was not a game I wanted to play for the rest of my business career.

This was further motivation to consider the idea of founding my own company. With the encouragement of my two best friends, Peter Copland and Don McGregor, I began formulating a plan to leave McGraw Hill and take my chances as an entrepreneur.

PART 3

THE HUME GROUP OF COMPANIES

Chapter 10

The Impossible Year

- - - - - - - -

In retrospect, my last year at McGraw Hill now seems impossible. I was committed to starting my own business, but couldn't resign my position at McGraw Hill until capital was raised to fund the new business, including a salary to cover my family's basic living costs. There could be no slacking off in handling my full time day job as I could not afford to lose it.

At that time I was enrolled at the University of Toronto's School of Business taking a certificate course in Business Administration. Classes were held two evenings each week. As well, there were homework assignments and preparing for exams. My classmates were on average 15 years younger and completing degree courses in business administration.

To arrange financing for the new business, a detailed business plan and financial projections had to be prepared. This was before Excel had been invented. It took weeks to build spreadsheets that can now be completed in hours. The most powerful tool available at the time was a hand held calculator.

Peter Copland's guidance was invaluable in preparing the business plan. He provided templates for the financial modeling, and how to write up a report on the company. Having recently raised funds for the founding of Chinook Chemicals, Peter knew what had to be done and how best to do it. His assistance shaved weeks off the time it would have taken without his help.

When completed, the business plan indicated we would have to raise a minimum of $300,000.

Of this amount, about $15,000 in angel financing was raised a single evening at a meeting with close friends and family, including Don and Peter, and members of an investment club. To this, I added $5,000 from my savings. With $20,000 in newly raised equity the business was incorporated as Coneducor Inc. This was a contraction of Continuing Education Corporation.

Before the required funding of $300,000 could be raised from the venture capital industry, a core management team had to be recruited. We had to have completed about 25% of the successful investing and money management course, and a Board of Advisors was needed to review the program, and endorse it in advertising to consumers.

About this time it was announced that Charles Neapole had recently retired as President of The Royal Bank of Canada. After tracking down his address and telephone number, I called Neapole's home, and he picked up the phone. After explaining the concept of a self-study program to teach the general public money management and investing skills, he immediately recognized the need for such a program. We met over lunch the following week and he agreed to Chair our Advisory Board. I was ecstatic.

With Charlie Neapole as the Chairman of Coneducor's Advisory Board we were in a much stronger position when approaching venture capital investors. He was also a great help in recruiting the various investing and money management experts who would provide the intellectual content for the course. As an unexpected bonus, Charlie arranged for the company to get a line of credit through the RBC.

Much of the contact work to recruit and manage the newly incorporated company had to be done during the day on McGraw Hill's time. This was an uncomfortable situation. Had I lost my job, it would have been disastrous. At one point Lorne Wilkinson, my boss at McGraw Hill, was abrupt with me and in a black mood during our weekly meetings. I was certain he had discovered, or was at least suspicious of my extra-curricular activities, and I was about to be fired. Living under this pressure was intolerable. I decided to confront the situation head on. At our next weekly meeting, I raised the issue of his dark moods when meeting with me, and asked if my job was at risk. His response was not what I expected. He said, "hell no, you're doing a great job. I should apologize to you." He confessed to having problems in his personal life that was affecting his interactions at work. I felt sorry for Lorne, but slept well that night.

That situation was a valuable lesson. When there is a perceived issue with a work colleague, it is best to address the situation head on.

Feeling more comfortable with my situation at McGraw Hill, work on the *Successful Investing and Money Management* course got underway in earnest.

I developed a course outline and templates for each lesson of the *Successful Investing and Money Management* self-study program. This work was done at home in the evenings, based on what I had learned during my week in Washington with the head of McGraw Hill's' distance education division.

With a detailed description of the course completed, I had to retain a professional journalist to write the twenty lessons. This was a major assignment. We were successful in recruiting one of Canada's leading business and investing columnists. He was introduced to me by Morty Shulman.

Before going after a $300,000 investment from venture capitalists, we needed to complete at least a third of the course.

Our writer was right on schedule for the first couple of months. Then he went silent and stopped providing updates. He would not return my calls. One hot June night at about 1:00 AM he called me on the verge of crying. It was not a good news call. He resigned from the project saying it was far more work than he could handle. He was out of his depth. With the message delivered, he hung up abruptly.

This was panic time. I had to find a replacement without delay. But where to begin? It had taken two months to find the original writer and there was no plan B.

Again, luck was with me. A day or so later, while reading the business section of our daily newspaper I came across an article announcing that the Government of Canada was disbanding a department that developed self-learning courses for government employees. Just maybe one of those being laid off was the writer we were looking for. With nothing to lose, and not much hope, I phoned the Government Information office in Ottawa and was referred to a David Cowan who headed up the department being disbanded.

We arranged a meeting for the next day. Within 15 minutes of meeting David it was clear my business Karma was in great shape. David knew exactly what had to be done to develop the Successful Investing and Money Management course. And he was available to start work on the project immediately.

David was a fascinating man. As an infant boiling water was accidently spilt over his entire face. This required numerous skin grafts over many years. Despite the extensive surgery his face was terribly scarred from ear to ear. At first it was difficult getting past the scarred face when talking with David. But he was an amazing man. He did not let his physical deformities hold him back. He had a warm smile and spoke gently and clearly. Within minutes you forgot about his face and focused on what he had to say. He had mastered the building of effective self-study programs. When David joined us, he developed the *Successful Investing and Money Management* using fusion of the pedagogical strategies he had developed for the Government of Canada with those employed by McGraw Hill. When it was published, our *Successful Investing and Money Management* program was, without a doubt, the best self-study program in North America. We quickly made up the time lost when our original writer packed it in.

Within a couple of months of David Cowan joining our team, we had completed about half of the *Successful Investing and Money Management* course, and we were ready to start meeting with venture capital companies. One of the first we approached was Helix Investments, owned by Ben Webster. He came from a family with major media interests. He was interested and brought one of his colleagues, Michael Needham, into the meeting. Later, when Helix invested in our company Needham joined our Board of Directors. Michael was a tall, rangy, charming, and as I would soon learn, a superb and aggressive squash player. He also understood how to get start-up companies up and running. Before moving forward with an investment, Helix wanted to see two things; another two years of financial forecasts based on US markets, and market research indicating there was a market for the Successful Investing and Money Management course. It was suggested that we hold a series of focus groups to learn how consumers felt about enrolling in a home study course on investing and money management.

Doing two more years of financial projections was a time consuming task, but not a problem. However, we had no funds to conduct focus groups.

Here's how that problem was resolved. The professor teaching my business accounting course at the University of Toronto was Peter McQuillan. Before teaching his evening classes, Peter usually had dinner at Swiss Chalet, a mid-range Canadian chain with a restaurant adjacent to the U of T campus. As it happened, I too ate at the same Swiss Chalet before attending his accounting classes.

The following week, on entering the Swiss Chalet, I walked up to his table and asked if I could join him.

Over dinner McQuillan was informed of my plans to develop the *Successful Investing and Money Management* course, and I asked him for small favor. At the end of his next class, would he agree to read a description of the course to his students, and ask how many would be interested in signing up for it. Peter agreed to conduct the survey, and give me a note confirming the results. That evening there were approximately 100 students in attendance. After seeing the survey results Peter commented, "You must be disappointed that only about a third of the class are interested in your course." In fact I was thrilled. The business would be a smashing success if only 2% of the adult population would enrol in the *Successful Investing and Money Management* course.

As he handed over the note reporting on the class survey results, another favor was asked of Peter McQuillan. Because my life was so busy, I was going to miss the deadline he'd set for handing in the term paper due at the end of his business finance course. I asked if the company report that had been done to raise capital for my new company could be submitted as the required term paper. Peter reluctantly agreed to this arrangement. He graded the paper as a "B". I had hoped for an A.

Peter McQuillan's off the cuff market research convinced Helix Investments to be our lead investor with a commitment to investment $150,000. And they agreed to actively help us to raise the additional $150,000 we'd need to complete the financing.

With assistance from Helix, we got commitments for the balance of the $300,000 from two sources; TD Capital and Dick Bonnycastle a venture capitalist from Calgary who owned the controlling interest in Harlequin Romances, a great romance publishing success story.

Upon making their investments, both Ben Webster and Dick Bonneycastle agreed to join Charles Neapole on our Advisory Board.

With the investment syndicate in place, a date was set when the financing was to close. It was agreed that all parties to the investment would have their checks to our lawyer's office by 11:00 AM on the day of the closing.

I arrived shortly before the closing time and was informed the investment from TD had not arrived, and was given a message to call them. On the callback, TD reported that after a further review of our financial projections they had come to the conclusion our shares were overpriced. TD would make the agreed to investment, but only if we the share price was lowered by 20%. I was in shell shock.

I reported this to the company's lawyer at Tory, Tory, Deslauriers and Bennington, and he was not so surprised. Apparently it was not uncommon for investors who knew one another to use this ruse to drive down the agreed to share price. But on this occasion that tactic failed.

Our lawyer called one of his clients, Bruce McLaughlin a wealthy real estate developer who had once fallen prey to this same tactic. McLaughlin was asked if he would be prepared to take up TD shares portion of the investment which was $70,000. He agreed. Moreover, he picked up the cab fare to have his check delivered to our lawyer's office in time to meet the closing deadline. We had survived a near disaster. My heart rate returned to normal when the checks were safely deposited in the company's bank account. Within a few months we found another investor to buy out McLaughlin's stake in the company.

With $300,000 in the Coneducor bank account, we had the money to fund our market launch.

A few weeks before, we reached an agreement with Goodis Goldberg and Soren to be the company's ad agency. At the time they were one of the hottest ad agencies in Canada. Their launch strategy was to run full page ads promoting the *Successful Investing and Money Management* course in leading Canadian financial and consumer publications. This campaign was to be launched the first week of January 1973. GGS predicted we would have about 250 enrollments in the course within a month of the launch.

During November and December of 1972, most of my evenings, and every weekend, were spent proof reading the twenty lesson course, laying out pages for the printer, and arranging to have 500 copies printed and delivered to the basement of my home. In January, when enrollments from GGS's sales campaign started to come in, we would mail lessons of the *Successful Investing and Money Management home study program* to each new enrollee at the rate of one every second week.

To help launch the company, Peter Copland provided Coneducor with a free office at the headquarters of his company Chinook Chemicals, in the heart of Toronto's business district.

Patricia Clark, my long time secretary at McGraw Hill agreed to join Coneducor at its launch to handle customer service operations. She was practical, efficient, and cool headed. A fortyish red head, she was always pleasant and could be counted on to be discreet. This was essential over the previous year when I was juggling my McGraw Hill's responsibilities with what had to be done during the day in connection with the launch of Coneducor.

1972 was a very nervous and exciting Christmas in the Hume Household. My wife Patricia and my kids Charron and Peter had been living with me through the wildly hectic past year. Although I had spent most of my evenings and weekend at home, this time was devoted almost exclusively on the launch of Coneducor. It had not been an easy time for my family. In retrospect, I now realize my family paid a heavy price.

Chapter 11

Two difficult births

January 1973 was a seminal date in my life. After twenty years of working for a big US owned company, I was leaving the security of a large well-established business to become an entrepreneur. Family and many close friends thought I had taken leave of my senses. Who would be dumb enough to leave a Group Vice-president position at McGraw Hill to found a company that was planning to develop and sell correspondence courses?

But I was convinced the world needed a self-study course that taught the average person how to manage money and make sound investments. These are crucial life skills not taught at school or at home. When parents awkwardly give their kids the bird and bees talk, at least they have some hands on experience with sex. But few working age adults have any meaningful training or experience in the vitally important topic of personal investing and money management.

I was taking a gigantic step launching this new business. At McGraw Hill, I was part of a well-established business with a dependable cash flow from thousands of long-term customers, proven effective business protocols for getting work done, a full range of support services including a place to work, funding for new product development, accounting services, and a wide range of highly trained colleagues to support me.

By founding Condeucor, I was leaving this well-established business ecosystem, and entering into a new world where I was entirely on my own. I had to create a new business from scratch. There was no instruction manual, no established business protocols, and no on-the-job training. There were no established employees to teach me the ropes. I was setting off into uncharted territory with only an unproven business plan to guide the way forward.

It requires nerves of steel and a never-give-up attitude to be an entrepreneur. You must have a high tolerance for risk and a high level of trust in your own abilities.

As businesses passes through the entrepreneurial stage, the management team evolves. Those who come on board during the post-entrepreneurial stage are less inclined to assume risks, and more interested in establishing a stable and highly efficient business.

Today we rarely give a thought to the highly competent men and women who manage an established companies manufacturing light bulbs, computers, or offering hospitality and medical services etc. We take them for granted. But we are still fascinated by the entrepreneurs such as Thomas Edison, Steve Jobs, Bill Gates and Elon Musk who converted ground breaking ideas and innovations into highly successful businesses that changed the world.

In no way am I in the same league as Edison, Gates, Musk, or Jobs, but I was born with an entrepreneurial gene. Is being an entrepreneur a curse or a blessing? I hope this memoir sheds light on what it means to choose the life of an entrepreneur. It was right for me, but it's not the best career choice for most women and men.

Being an entrepreneur has given meaning to my life. The *Successful Investing and Money Management* self-study program I developed taught millions of people how to manage their money wisely and gain financial independence, and The Hume Group of companies provided good jobs for hundreds of people.

For me, being an entrepreneur had a darker side too. My children didn't get the attention they deserved, my marriage ended in divorce, and some of those who invested in the businesses I founded lost money.

My theory on the need for a successful investing and money management course was based on solid evidence. Over the previous three years two books I had published while at McGraw Hill had served as the market research for the company I was planning. Bill Reddin's *Money Book* had become an underground Canadian best-seller, and *Morton Shulman's Anyone Can Make a Million* reached #1 on US and Canadian best-seller lists.

However, within a few months of launching Coneducor it looked like the critics who questioned my decision to leave McGraw Hill had got it right. Coneducor came within a hair of going down in flames. Two years later, I founded a US company and, it too stumbled out of the starting gate.

Here are the near death experiences of my first two start-ups.

The skills acquired through my McGraw Hill experience were vitally important in enabling me to develop the *Successful Investing and Money Management* self-study program. To market the course we retained one of Canada's top-ranked advertising agencies, Goodis, Goldberg and Sorin. Initially Coneducor's customer service operations would be handled from my home.

To launch the *Successful Investing and Money Management* course in Canada Goodis Goldberg and Soren (GGS), placed full-page ads in *The Financial Post, Canadian Business, Toronto Life Magazine*, and a few other general interest magazines. The budget for this marketing launch was $100,000. This represented about a third of the funds we had raised to found the company.

To enrol in the *Successful Investing and Money Management* course, consumers would clip out a coupon at the lower-right corner of the ad, fill in their name and address, write out a check for the $10 registration fee, place the coupon and check in envelope addressed to Coneducor's office, and drop the envelope in the nearest post box.

Goodis Goldberg and Sorin provided a forecast estimating that their ad campaign for the *Successful Investing and Money Management* course would generate 200 to 300 enrolments within the first 30 days.

For the launch, I had arranged to take an extended Christmas holiday from my job at McGraw Hill.

This holiday time was spent setting up an office and developing procedures for processing new enrolments in the *Successful Investing and Money Management* course. As well, Patricia Clark the company's first and at that time only employee, had to be trained and ready to handle the administrative side of the business. The course materials were being printed and delivered to my at-home warehouse, ready for shipping as new enrollments began coming in. A distribution and warehousing system had to be set up in the basement of my home.

When the holiday was over, I would return to McGraw Hill and tender my resignation. That was the plan. At the time it seemed sensible. Even if we missed the GGS sales target by 50%, there would be sufficient capital to launch a follow-up sales campaign.

Enrollments were expected to start coming in during the second week of January. It was an exciting time as we set up and organized the new Condeducor offices. It was exhilarating to think that all the work and planning over the past 18-months was about to bear fruit.

But two weeks after the first Successful Investing and Money Management ads appeared, the postman had delivered just eleven enrollments. The launch was an utter disaster.

An emergency meeting was arranged with the senior partners at Goodis Goldberg and Soren. They were stunned. I was devastated. GGS had no clue of where to go from here. They had no plan B. At the end of the meeting GGS was dismissed on the spot.

This was one of the worst days of my life. Despite the disastrous launch, I'd not lost faith in in the *Successful Investing and Money Management* course. Based on my experience at McGraw Hill, I knew there were tens of thousands of hard working people who wanted to learn how to protect and grow their hard earned income.

Going home after the GGS meeting, I was an emotional basket case. But I could not lose control. Failure was not an option. A way forward must be found. It was important to stay cool and think clearly. The full extent of the disastrous marketing launch couldn't be revealed to my wife or investors until there was a plan in place to salvage the situation.

To cap off the worst possible start-up, the next day I had to return to McGraw Hill at the conclusion of my holiday. Considering the disastrous launch of the *Successful Investing and Money Management* course, it was my plan to continue working with McGraw Hill until we could sorted out Con-educor's future, if there was to be one.

My hope of continuing to work for McGraw Hill was dashed before reaching my office. When I returned from my holiday, my boss Lorne Wilkinson was waiting for me. He asked me to come into his office — immediately. Before I had time to take off my coat he said, *"This has got be yours. Is it?"* He pointed to the most recent issue of *The Financial Post*, laid out on his desk. It was opened to the full page *Successful Investing and Money Management* ad. He spat out, "If you are behind this, clean out your desk right now". Lorne was an angry man.

Of course I fessed up and reminded Lorne that McGraw Hill had passed on the project. The course had been developed on my own time, and I had always received high marks in carrying out my McGraw Hill responsibilities.

I hated leaving under these circumstances. The company had been good to me. Everything I knew about publishing and business management was learned during my years at McGraw Hill. They had given me the opportunity grow and achieve success. Furthermore, I enjoyed working with my boss Lorne, the company's President John McMillan, and my General Book Division team.

It was a sad day saying goodbye to McGraw Hill. And yet there was a feeling of freedom, and the excitement that comes when moving on to explore exciting new opportunities.

There was one bit of comforting news coming out of the day. My severance package from McGraw Hill gave my family some financial breathing room to work out how to move forward with Coneducor.

Now, with McGraw Hill in the rear mirror, I had to find a new ad agency immediately. This was an urgent issue. To start the search, it seemed reasonable to look for an agency representing other clients selling intellectual properties. In leafing through magazines several *Reader's Digest* ads caught my attention. They were selling book series by running ads in their own publications, and magazines they did not own. If *Reader's Digest* could successfully sell books directly to consumers, surely we could use the same tactics to sell the *Successful Investing and Money Management course.*

Several months earlier, I had chatted with a *Reader Digest's* marketing executive at a publishing conference and he gave me his business card. His name was Tony Keenan. I gave him a call that day. After hearing my tale of woe, Tony gave me a ten-minute primer on direct-to-consumer mass marketing.

Tony explained that most conventional advertising, as done by Goodis Goldberg and Soren, was used to drive consumers to retail outlets. The sales are closed at the retail location through in store displays and with the assistance of on the floor sales reps.

Direct-to-consumer mass marketing is a vastly different business. It requires the same expertise used by ad agencies to create interest in a product or service. But that is only half the battle. *Direct-to-consumer mass marketers must also be highly skilled at closing sales on the spot.* There is another big difference. All elements of a sophisticated direct-to-consumer marketing campaign are pre-tested before committing to a major roll out.

This approach to marketing sounded right-on-the mark, and excited me. I'd learned something new and important that day: The need to conduct extensive testing before rolling out a major marketing campaign. All elements should be tested including alternative sales messaging and headlines, the media that was used to generate sales, price, and offer alternatives. None of this testing had been carried out by GGS.

Despite my success with McGraw Hill Direct Mail department, testing was a new concept to me. There was much I had to learn about direct-to-consumer mass marketing.

When GGS was retained, I wasn't aware there were agencies specializing in direct-to-consumer mass marketing. Tony Keenan advised me that one of the best was Wunderman

Direct. They were headquartered in New York with a Canadian office in Montreal.

At Tony Keenan's recommendation, I called Alan Booth, a senior executive at Wunderman's office in Montreal. After an extensive telephone briefing on the *Successful Investing and Money Management* course, Booth was intrigued and agreed to fly to Toronto the next day. After a careful review of the course, and the scope of the market for those interested in learning investing and money management skills, he was convinced there was a solid market for the program. Alan suggested the best way to reach this market was through precisely targeted direct mail marketing.

Booth was a tall sandy haired Scott in his mid-30s. He spoke with the calm assurance of someone with deep knowledge of direct-to-consumer mass marketing. He suggested we set up a small direct mail test to get a statistically reliable assessment of the market sectors most interested in signing up for the *Successful Investing and money Management* course. As well, this would enable us test two different sales pitches, and the fees being charged to enrol in the course.

The sales campaign created by Goodis, Goldberg, and Sorin involved no testing. No wonder they had no plan B when their marketing plan failed so resoundingly.

Within a few days, Booth delivered Wunderman's proposal for a direct mail marketing test. The budget was $30,000. The mailing lists to be tested included doctors, dentists, and subscribers to financial and investing publications, including *Money Magazine* and *The Financial Post*. Doctors and dentists were the only professions singled out for the test.

They had been selected because of their relatively high incomes and because mailing lists with their home address were readily available.

In total, the combined mailing lists selected for the Wunderman direct mail test represented a mailing universe of 300,000 individuals. Initially we would run marketing tests to ten percent of the available names. If our testing indicated that only half of the total mailing universe generated an acceptable response rate of 1.5%, we had a solid business. Assuming a roll out to the balance of the 150,000 names, at the same response rate, this would generate more than 1,500 *Successful Investing and Money Management* enrollees. We would have a successful business.

After a careful assessment of Wunderman's test proposal I was quickly falling in love with direct-to-consumer mass marketing. This form of marketing is highly controlled enabling the marketer to simultaneously test all key variables in a marketing program before rolling it out to the entire market. The best performing combination of media, messaging, and price can be combined to minimize the risk of failure and amplify the likelihood of success when rolling out to the most responsive mailing lists. It was fascinating to see how this marketing strategy relied on a fusion of creativity and scientific precision to achieve clear cut goals.

Over the next few days, I reviewed the Wunderman test proposal several times and marvelled at the logic involved in this marketing discipline. I made a commitment to myself that one day Coneducor would be a leader in the field of direct-to-consumer mass marketing. To learn more about this fascinating discipline I joined the *Canadian Direct Marketing Association* and enrolled in their "introduction to direct marketing" seminars.

Another issue needed to be addressed: The Wunderman team were adamant that the name of the company needed to be changed. GGS had made a similar comment. There were concerns that the Coneducor name might leave the impression that the services offered may be a "con" job. I wasn't going to argue with these observation. The decision was made to re-brand the company.

To handle the re-branding, we reached out to Robert Burns. Robert was one of the day's hottest designers of corporate logos with offices in Toronto and New York. He loved the concept of a self-study course to teach money management and investing skills and agreed to take on the assignment. Robert suggested we change the company name to Hume Publishing. He made the point that people have more confidence in a company where the owner is identified. But there was a big problem. The fee quoted by Robert Burn's was $50,000. Our budget was $5,000.

Robert explained that when working with big corporations, it takes weeks to work up a number of branding alternatives that can be presented for the consideration of company's senior management and board of directors. Then, the final decision on a re-branding had to go through numerous committees and tweaking before the final design was approved and developed. As a small start-up company we didn't need to go through this complex branding exercise, and I wanted Burns. So I made him this offer: Take two days to come up with a single new name and logo design, and we'll pay you $5,000. He accepted the challenge, and within 48 hours he came up with the Hume Publishing name, and this logo.

Wunderman was delighted with the new name and logo, as was I.

The timing of our direct mail test was now an issue. It would take about two months to create the campaign, and another month to do the printing and mailing. This meant we had to find the money, not only to run the direct mail campaign, but also to cover the company overheads for up to four months.

We approached the manager of the Royal Bank of Canada requesting a $30,000 line of credit. Knowing that Charles Neapole, their recently retired President, was the Chairman of Hume Publishing's Advisory Board, the bank manager assigned Mr. Neapole's son Bill to assess our loan application. This was the first time I realized Charlie's son worked at the RBC branch we were using. Within days, the line of credit was approved. This would never happen in today's strictly regulated banking industry.

I was now living on tenterhooks. If this test didn't pan out, the company would not survive. I would be unemployed after throwing away a Group Vice-president position at McGraw Hill.

Sleep was impossible. During the day, seconds dragged on like hours. Days passed like months. But buckling under the pressure wasn't an option. Deep down I knew there were tens of thousands of individuals who would sign up for a course on *Successful Investing and Money Management*. And, I felt a high level of confidence in Wunderman's direct-to-consumer mass marketing strategy.

Finally, our direct mail was designed, printed and delivered to the post office.

Then, exactly 10 days later, the postman arrived at our office carrying a hand full of reply envelopes from our direct mail test.

The first envelope was ripped open by my assistant Patricia without taking the time to reach for a letter opener. Shaking it, two enrollments in the *Successful Investing and Money Management* course fell to her desk top. Two dentists operating from the same office had enrolled. That day we had our first five enrollments from the direct mail program.

We celebrated by ordering in pizza for lunch.

Over the next three weeks we generated 58 orders from the direct mail test. This was a response rate of almost 2%. The highest responders were doctors and dentists. 2.5% of them who received our direct mail packages signed up for the *Successful Investing and Money Management* course. This exceeded our most optimistic forecast.

With a proven effective marketing strategy, Hume Publishing was now on its way to becoming North America's leading publisher of consumer home-study programs. Over the next two years, working with Wunderman Direct as our ad agency, Hume Publishing grew steadily, picking up momentum as the months rolled by.

We moved to a new office/distribution facility in suburban Toronto and began getting publicity and good reviews of the *Successful Investing and Money Management* course. These began showing up mostly in the business sections of daily newspapers. I was invited to be interviewed on *The Money Show*, a popular show in the Toronto by CITY TV. During this, my first TV interview, I nervously swivelled my chair from side to side. It got so bad the interviewer, Manny Batler, had to reach over and put his foot on my chair to keep me swivelling in and out of the picture.

At this point, the major constraint to the growth of Hume Publishing was how to fund our direct mail marketing rollout program. After wasting $100,000 on the futile GGS marketing launch, we had no cash reserve and had to grow from the cash flow generated on a month-to-month basis.

Canada's 120,000 doctors and dentists remained by far our best customers. If only there were more of them. And there were more, many more when we were ready to tackle the US market. Ten times more!

To generate incremental income during this cash strapped period, I approached the President of the Canadian Direct Marketing Association (CDMA), and suggested we publish a CDMA self-study course on direct-to-consumer marketing. With the help of Alan Booth and our Wunderman association, we successfully negotiated $50,000 contract to develop the course. The CDMA were pleased with the direct-response marketing course they had commissioned from Hume Publishing. The fees earned from this contact went directly to the funding of direct mail marketing campaigns.

In working with the CDMA, the association's president and I developed a solid bond, and he asked me to serve on the CDMA's board. This honor was readily accepted. I continued as a board member for several years.

In 1975, with Hume Publishing's Canadian business growing steadily, it was time to look south and launch a US subsidiary. As was the case in Canada, our US launch did not go as planned. It too came within a hair of being declared a still birth. Here's the story.

Our research had established there was no US competitor to the *Successful Investing and Money Management* self-study program. And there were ten times more doctors and dentists in the US than in Canada. After completing a business plan for the US market, we needed to arrange the necessary funding of $300,000. Based on our success in Canada, our original investment syndicate agreed to finance the US launch

Hume Publishing's first US office was set up in Ann Arbor, Michigan. This location was chosen because it is just a four hour drive from Toronto and near a major university. This was important because many of the consultants contributing to the *Successful Investing and Money Management* course were university professors, and much of the course content had to be adapted for the US market.

Because doctors and dentists were our best customers, it seemed a slam dunk that we would make money in the US right out of the gate by focusing on these markets for the launch. Accordingly, 80% of the initial 100,000 direct mail pieces sent out in the US launch went to doctors and dentists. The other twenty percent went to subscribers of publication including *Money Magazine* and *The Wall Street Journal*.

To get the US operation up and running, we recruited a skeleton staff of two in the Ann Arbor office, and one employee was employed to handle the distribution of course materials from a small rented warehouse space. Here we stocked a supply of loose leaf binders and printed course materials that would go to new US enrollees *in Successful Investing and Money Management*. The newly appointed manager of the Ann Arbor office visited Toronto for two weeks of training.

Based on our Canadian experience, we were expecting to generate between 750 and 1500 enrollments during the first month of the US launch. Two of our core admin staff in Toronto, Elspeth Kean from our accounting staff, and our first employee Patricia Clark, agreed to spend a month living at a Holiday Inn in Ann Arbor. They would train the US staff and handle the initial rush of new enrollments. I drove to Ann Arbor to be there when the initial US orders were expected to start coming in.

We drank endless cups of coffee and waited in great excitement for the mailman to arrive bearing bags full of US *Successful Investing and Money Management* enrollees. We worried that our skeleton staff may not have the capacity to handle all of the work, should the launch generate more enrollments than forecasted.

When enrollments from our US launch finally started coming in, it was not in a sudden surge we couldn't handle.

The postman arrived with only a small handful of envelopes. Our Ann Arbor office manager suggested that something must be amiss with the postal system. Not to worry, they'll have it sorted out in a few days. Maybe tomorrow with get an entire mail bag of *Successful Investing and Money Management* enrollments. After two more days of receiving only a few enrollments, the manager of our Ann Arbor office became concerned and took a trip to the local post office to learn what was holding up the mail. She returned dejected.

There was no backlog of mail at the post office. US Post was doing a great job. We had to accept the fact that our US launch was a failure.

It was a black day in Ann Arbor for the Hume Publishing team. That evening we met over dinner at the Holiday Inn for a post mortem. The shabby dining room overlooked a run-down swimming pool and smelled of chlorine. This matched our mood. The food was what you'd expect in a second rate Holiday Inn. Rather than Champagne, we drank too much beer. Next morning at 10:00 we would meet to begin an autopsy on the failed US direct mail test.

Upon arriving at the office the next morning, there was an urgent message to call the president of the Chicago based company that supplied the three ring binders that go to each new enrollee in the *Successful Investing and Money Management* course. This guy wasn't calling to wish us good luck with our launch. It seems we were overdue in paying their invoice and, if it was not paid by the end of the week, our account was going to a collection agency. This call further blackened my already dark mood.

RONALD HUME

But, within a half hour of beginning an autopsy on the failed direct mail program we discovered the patient wasn't quite dead.

There was no doubt about it. Results from doctors and dentists were awful. In Canada, we were routinely generating response rates in excess of 2% from docs and dentists. In the US test, they were coming in at less than a quarter of one percent. It would take several days to figure out why. But the response rates from subscribers to *Money Magazine* and *The Wall Street Journal* were right on budget.

This was good news. In the US, there are many more subscribers to *Money Magazine, The Wall Street Journal*, and similar publications than there are doctors and dentists.

To learn why doctors and dentists in the US responded so poorly, we contacted Wunderman's New York office. The explanation was simple. With no public health care system, doctors and dentists in the US were earning almost twice the income of their Canadian counterparts, and had far more discretionary income to invest. As a consequence a high percentage of US doctors and dentists retain professional wealth managers. The same phenomenon occurs at all income levels in all market sectors. For instance, low income car owners do their own auto repair and maintenance work. Those with higher incomes use a licensed auto mechanic.

We learned one important lessons from this test. Before doing any test marketing be sure to have local knowledge when setting up the test parameters.

Despite the poor results from doctors and dentists, the marketing tests conducted to *Wall Street Journal* and *Money*

Magazine subscribers established that we had a viable business in the US.

The day ended with another positive development. During a chat with our Ann Arbor warehouse employee while he was fulfilling orders, we noticed a 3-ring binders supplied by the cranky Chicago supplier had a slit in its spine. Checking other binders from the same carton, we found that about 20% of them had similar slits. Together, we checked a half dozen more cartons and found they all contained several defective binders.

The manager of our Ann Arbor office placed a call to the binder company's president advising him of the situation, and demanding he pick up his defective merchandise.

What started as a day from hell ended on a high note. Our direct marketing test confirmed there was a strong US market for the *Successful Investing and Money Management* course.

We were on the way!

Chapter 12

Building the Engine Room

- - - - - - - - -

By now it was clear the future of Hume Publishing was highly dependent on the company's direct-to-consumer mass marketing capabilities. It was equally obvious the key to success in this discipline is testing. Every element of a direct mail campaign must be tested before rolling out to the full target market.

To set up and manage a large-scale mass marketing direct response program was a time consuming procedure. With dozens of tests taking place simultaneously, it would take more hours that there are in a day to read and evaluate each test cell manually. This limited the amount of testing we could do, and slowed down our capability to roll out fast when a new and more effective creative approach, or an effective new marketing media was identified through the testing.

To optimize the effectiveness of the company's marketing, we planned to develop an automated marketing management system. The system would turn out daily reports providing our marketing team with the ability to immediately evaluate the effectiveness of each marketing program in real time, and provide immediate results on each marketing test.

In consultation with our Wunderman colleagues we worked out the parameters we wanted to build into the system. These included:

1. Providing at a glance information on the effectiveness of each specific advertising campaign by media. Pre-internet these were direct mail, newspaper ads, TV, radio, on-page ads in newspapers and magazines, and paid inserts in newspapers and magazines.

2. Measuring the effectiveness of headlines and sub-heads used to attract the immediate attention of prospective buyers

3. Measuring the effectiveness of advertising copy that closes the sale.

4. Having immediate feedback on the optimum price and offer combinations being tested. Offers may involve term payments or money back guaranties.

5. Knowing the response curve of orders received through each specific media. For example when sending out a direct mail campaign, half of the response come in within approximately 10 days of the first order. With newspapers, most of are received within 24 hours. By knowing response rate curves on the hundreds of active sales campaigns, we could rapidly convert up-coming ad campaigns to the best performing advertising sales copy and pricing. This was the "control" against which all

tests are measured. Having accurate forecasts of upcoming sales make it possible to control inventory and manufacturing volumes.

6. Understanding seasonality sales trends. With most products and services sales volumes vary widely throughout the year. These month-to-month variances often exceed 200% from the best to the worst months.

7. Knowing the "sales cost ratio" of each active marketing campaign was a key metric to be monitored on a daily basis. This single number indicated the success each campaign.

By developing an automated testing system with these capabilities the company could grow faster, and operate more profitably. Here how: by running tests in each of these seven categories, where the best performing test cells out-performed the average by just 5%, the cumulative sales increase would be about 40% on a roll out. At an average increase of 10%, the cumulative sales increase is almost 200%. And these additional sales are achieved with NO INCREASE in media costs. Even today, most marketing professionals remain unaware that the success of their mass marketing initiatives are subject to the magic of compounding.

One of the most neglected areas of testing is measuring the relative effectiveness of the advertising copy and headlines. The first time I was involved in a test where only the headline in a full page newspaper ad was changed, the response rate increased by 240%. Over my 20 years in the mass marketing business, I have met no one who can consistently pick the winner in head-to- head copy tests. The only way to what works, and what does not, is through disciplined testing.

Many marketing professionals rely on focus groups to test alternative sales copy or headlines. In my experience, focus groups participants will offer opinions to make themselves look good, or to make the group moderator feel good. With direct mail or email tests you get 100% reliable information on an ads effectiveness. The same applies when testing price and offer alternatives.

When Hume Publishing was launched, no software was available to manage a sophisticated direct-to-consumer mass marketing program. It was my goal to develop a proprietary automated marketing system for Hume Publishing.

For advice on how to build a mass marketing management software system, I contacted Bill Baker. He had been McGraw Hill's VP Operations when the company built a new distribution center in Scarborough, Ontario.

Before joining McGraw Hill, Bill was a sales engineer with Honeywell's Electronic Processing Division. After his success at McGraw Hill, he was recruited by Nelson Canada, a major Canadian book publisher, as their Vice-President Operations and Information Systems.

Bill was fortyish, about six feet tall, with short cropped salt and pepper hair. Mild mannered, soft spoken, and articulate, you had the feeling Bill knew how to get things done, and done right.

To get Bill's insights on the viability to building an automated mass marketing system, I invited him to attend an upcoming weekend think tank of the Hume Publishing management team. It was taking place on a late autumn weekend at Sherwood Inn in Muskoka. He accepted and his contribution to the weekend discussion was invaluable.

While driving home with Bill after the weekend at Sherwood, I asked if he knew anyone the capabilities required to design and build a mass marketing management software system. No one came to mind. He promised to make some calls to see if any of the engineers he had worked with at Honeywell may be available.

Over the weekend, I learned something about Bill I would never have suspected. He was not particularly pleased with his Vice-President Operations role at Nelson.

Based on this information, I thought why not offer Bill the Vice-President Operations role at Hume Publishing All he can is say no, and just maybe he'd say yes.

I discussed this with my wife Penny and Bill Vernon our VP marketing who had attended the Sherwood Inn meeting. It was their feeling that Bill would be insulted by suggesting he resign from a senior management role at one of Canada's major publishing company to join a small start-up.

After thinking about this for a few days, I decided to offer the job to Bill. The worst that could happen is he would feel insulted. On the other hand, he just might say yes. As I've learned, if you don't ask you don't get.

The next day I gave Bill a call to see if he had come up with anyone with the know-how to build a mass marketing management software system. No one had come to mind.

Half-jokingly I said. "Why don't you take it on?" Working with us may be more fun than you are having at Nelson. After a moment's hesitation he said, "I'd consider that."

Over the next few days, we worked out a deal, and Bill joined Hume Publishing as VP Operations in January 1981. I was ecstatic!

Over my entire career, Bill was the single best executive I ever worked with. Upon joining Hume Publishing, his mission was to set up and manage state-of-the art Canadian and US distribution centers, and build a mass marketing management software system. The system designed by Bill exceeded our expectations. It had the ability to split off test panels from a unique input group and test back-end variations such as shipping intervals, credit limits, packaging, etc.

Bill added another important element to our software's capabilities. It had the capability to manage the circulation system for Hume's newsletters, and link customers who were receiving both self-study programs and newsletters so that we could analyze relationships and cross-promote to all clients.

The unique aspect of The Hume Direct Marketing Software was its capability for turning out daily marketing analysis and reporting.

To build this multi-functional operating system, the company acquired an IBM System/38 computer at a cost over $350,000. (Hume was one the first companies in both Toronto and Atlanta to use these IBM systems). Bill later upgraded to an AS/400 IBM series 3 main-frame computer. Purchasing these computers required the building of dedicated air conditioned rooms with special flooring. Bill then assembled a team of five programmers who worked for the best part of a year writing the system's operating code.

This was a massive undertaking. Developing this management software system was the equivalent a moon landing for the direct marketing industry.

Each line of code had to be checked on a stand-alone basis, then integrated into the entire system. This required weeks of testing and de-bugging. After weeks of anxious waiting, Bill announced the system was ready for a live test.

When the day arrived you could hear the clicked, clack, clicked clack, as the printer spewed out the first comprehensive sales report. They were printed out in a continuous form 15 inches wide with 14 columns of the information. In the right hand column, you could read each individual sales campaign's sales sales/cost ratio and know at a glance it profitability.

As the marketing team began pouring over the reports, you could hear excited comments coming thick and fast. Here are a few I remember.

"Oh my g-d, Stu Maltin's new copy is beating Garry's by over 30%. I've gotta change to Stu's before we start to print the next batch of FSIs due at the printers next week."

"Come and look at this. The half-life on direct mail is just 8 days. I'd always assumed it was two weeks".

"Remember that test campaign to Forbes Magazine subscribers that we thought might be throwing money away? Well it's coming in at a sales ratio of almost 4:1. Let's get a campaign going to their full subscriber list next week, it'll be a big winner".

To better understand the power of Hume Publishing's proprietary mass marketing system, here are actual samples excerpted from the January 4 1990 marketing intake report:

Example 1: *Actual results from a price test conducted in January 1990*

The audience was 42,000 individuals taking self-study language courses

> *Half were offered the control price of $10 per lesson*
> *Half were offered a 15% reduction from the control price*

The response rate for the control price offer was:	*3.05%*
The response rate with a 15% price reduction was:	*2.15%*
This result: the lower price depressed response rates by	*29.50%*

Example 2: *Results from a copy test conducted January 1990*

The test media was a free standing insert

The audience was 44,400 subscribers to The Financial Times

> *Half received a promotional piece written by copywriter MW*
> *Half received a promotional piece written by copywriter TM*

The response rate for MW's package was:	*2.72%*
For TM's package it was:	*3.25%*
This test confirmed that TM's copy out-pulled MW's by	*15.80%*

From the day Hume Publishing's mass marketing management software system went live, the company's sales grew exponentially. By the mid-80s the company's revenues were over $40 million per year. (About $100 million today)

Without a doubt, the most important factor in Hume Publishing's success was the marketing software developed by Bill Baker and his team.

As well, Bill designed and operated a superbly efficient 30,000 square feet warehouse and distribution center based in suburban Atlanta. By the mid-80s this facility was distributing 25.000 packages per week.

A true believer in the *Successful Investing and Money Management* course, Bill completed it and applied what he learned to build a sizable nest egg and a comfortable life.

Chapter 13

Teaching the World
How To Build Wealth

- - - - - - - -

Hume Publishing was founded on a simple premise. Most people, regardless of their current status, want to be better off financially. Today students are willing to assume enormous personal debts to gain an education that will lead to a high paying job. *But they receive virtually no education on how the manage the money they earn. This is an absurd situation.*

In developing the *Successful Investing and Money Management* course, we wanted to teach the world how to manage the money they earned to be debt free as soon as possible, and make shrewd investments. If, through a Hume Publishing self-study program, we could teach an individual how to free up an additional $1,000 per year, and invest this at an average return of 5% over a working career of 40 years, that would amount to a nest egg of $1,989,564.58 when it came time to retire.

The first edition of the *Successful Investing and Money Management* course was designed and developed based on the self-study pedagogical tactics acquired during my

RONALD HUME

McGraw Hill years. This was further enhanced with the help of David Cowan who had spent his career designing self-study programs for the Government of Canada.

We recruited subject specialists in various areas of personal investing, money management, and insurance to provide the course content. Each subject specialist was a leading authority in their field and received a credit when the *Successful Investing and Money Management* course was published.

We employed a senior freelance writer to incorporate the investing and money management expertise provided by the subject specialists into a standard lesson template that included practice exercises. These exercises were designed to enable those taking a course to immediately apply what they were learning to improve their current financial situation.

When the first edition of *Successful Investing and Money Management* was developed, the layout and design was done on the kitchen table of my home, after my kids Charron and Peter went to bed. The table had to be cleared when my work wrapped up each evening. My wife Patricia insisted that there could be no signs of my clandestine work when Charron and Peter came to the kitchen for breakfast the next morning. At the time they were seven and eight years old.

Looking back to this period, my family was being neglected. My time was committed to two things; doing my job at McGraw Hill, and launching the new business. There was no time left to just hang out or play with my kids and my wife. Based on discussions with other entrepreneurs, this same situation is often the case especially during the initial launch phase of a new business.

It was a thrilling day for my wife and kids when the first edition of *Successful Investing and Money Management* was delivered to our home "warehouse and distribution center". The sturdy navy blue 3 ring binders that stored the course lessons looked slick and professional, and the individual lessons were engaging and easy-to-read. The whole family celebrated. My wife made mac and cheese for dinner, accompanied by a nice Merlo for Pat and me, and chocolate milk for Charron and Peter. For the first time my family could touch and feel the course that had consumed my life for the past year.

As new enrollments arrived at the office, they would be taken home that same evening and fulfilled from the ping pong table in our recreation room that same evening. Charron and Peter took delight in helping with the packaging and labeling. The packages would be dropped off at the Markham post office on my drive to work the next morning. This system worked well until we did the first rollout of a direct mail marketing campaign. The first twenty or so enrolments from that marketing campaign came in on a Friday. That evening, Charron Peter and I worked well past their bedtime on the packaging and labeling.

The next morning was Saturday and Charron and Peter came along to help me deliver the course shipments to the local post office. When we arrived at Markham's small village post office the postmaster informed us our twenty packages exceeded the limit he was authorized to process. We would have to travel into the city a drop them off at a commercial postal station. The next week we began the search for a new and bigger office/ warehouse.

At that time, we could never have imagined that by the time Charron and Peter were in high school, Hume Publishing would be shipping course material to 25,000 individuals each week from a 30,000 square foot warehouse in suburban Atlanta.

Because of the high profile *Financial Advisory Board* featured in our advertising, the general business media in Canada started to take notice of the *Successful Investing and Money Management* course, and we were delighted to get some early positive reviews. I was concerned that our extensive mass marketing program might attract competition from big companies such as International Correspondence Schools, *Reader's Digest* or *Time Life*.

The only way to protect against this threat was to continually up-date and improve all Hume Publishing self-study programs. This would be essential to build and sustain Hume Publishing's reputation as the Mercedes or Cadillac brand in our niche.

Student drop-out rates are the single most important factor in determining the customer satisfaction of a self-study program. Our goal was to keep dropouts to a maximum of 20%. Because those enrolling in Hume self-study courses could drop out any time with no penalty, we took these steps to minimize dropouts.

Successful Investing and Money Management and all Hume self-study programs were updated at each new printing. This enabled us to clarify any sections of a course where feedback from enrolees disclosed problems in understand concepts being taught, or in applying what they were learning.

As well, all economic data such as interest or mortgage rates were regularly updated. We offered a free counselling service. When enrollees had a problem understanding or applying what they were learning, they could arrange a telephone coaching session. Most of the course updates were based on input from our councillors. The delivery sequence of lessons was tested to determine those most engaging to enrollees. By delivering the most engaging lessons up front, dropouts could be reduced significantly during the first 6 – 8 lessons. If an enrollee got past these first half dozen lessons, dropouts dropped off dramatically. Our automated mass marketing software was invaluable in testing the optimum lesson sequencing. On a regular basis, we received feedback from teachers and academics complaining of the illogical sequencing of lessons. Maybe their own courses would have been more successful had they followed our model for sustaining student engagement. To increase the revenue per enrollee, we began adding new lessons to the *Successful Investing and Money Management* course. Within a few years, it grew from a 20 to a 30 lesson self-study program.

In the early days of Hume Publishing, we would look for ways to bootstrap new product development. At that time, we didn't have the funds or trained editorial staff to create new self-study courses from scratch. Instead, we sought out opportunities to acquire the rights to educational programs that could be easily adapted to our self-study template. We were successful on two occasions.

One day while skimming through *The Financial Post's* business section, I came across a small ad under the heading "businesses for sale". This immediately caught my eye because the business was a home-study course on Investing in Real Estate. This was worth checking out and a meeting was set up for early the next week with the business owner who lived in Ottawa.

He was a real estate broker, who had made a fortune in real estate and felt there was even more money to be made teaching others the real estate investment tactics he'd acquired over his twenty year career. He took me to his garage, opened the door, and there, stacked in neat plies were 500 thick red binders, each filled with about 400 pages of dense text material set in a small font size.

The owner admitted that, although he knew how to do profitable real estate deals, his expertise did not extend to designing or selling home-study courses. He was convinced there were tens of thousands who were seeking this valuable expertise, but over the past six months, he had sold fewer that twenty. He wanted someone to take the whole thing off his hands for $50,000, or about half the investment he had laid out in developing and printing the course.

He gave me two copies to review. Over the next couple of days, my time was consumed reviewing the course. The content was impressive, but there was no pedagogical framework, and it was poorly packaged. It had the look and feel of a long boring book, set in an undersized font that was not easy to read. No one was going to pay $100 for a self-study program with the look and feel of a huge hard-to-read 500 page book.

The next day, I made arrangements to have the course reviewed by a professional real estate investor. He got back to me confirming the basic content was valuable, but poorly presented. He complained of getting eye strain reading the lessons

Based on this assessment, we offered to pay the developer a royalty of 10% for the copyright to his course, with a maximum royalty payout capped at $75,000. The seller complained we were offering no up-front cash, but a few days later he accepted the offer. It's my guess we were the only offer he had.

Within three months, for an out of pocket investment of less than $10,000, we re-formatted the real estate investing content into a slick twenty lesson, *Successful Real Estate Investing* self-study program. We did this by using the same pedagogical template developed for the *Successful Investing and Money Management* course.

For a relatively small upfront investment, we had an almost instant ready to sell self-study program.

Over the next 15 years, we enrolled over 250,000 clients in the *Successful Real Estate Investing* self-study program. The Realtor who sold it was happy too. His royalty of $75,000 was paid in full within two years. He must have had a great bonfire with 500 copies of the course he printed and was unable to sell.

Within six months, a similar opportunity arose. One of Canada's largest trust companies was referred to me as someone who may be interested in acquiring a *Small Business Management* self-study program they had developed. Unfortunately, the trust company executive that developed the course, did not have a plan or a budget for promoting it to their small business clients. When senior management became aware of the situation, they approached me to see if Hume Publishing might be interested in acquiring the rights. We jumped at the opportunity. We were able to acquire the *Small Business Management* self-study program in return for a capped royalty. We had no up-front costs, other than re-branding the course.

This too was a great investment for Hume. As with the *Successful Real Estate Investing* course, this too generated 50,000 plus enrollments per year on an ongoing basis.

The next new product we developed, was a departure from self-study programs and required no major product development cost.

Twice a year, our management team held weekend think tanks at a resort in Muskoka. On these weekend getaways, it was my habit to take an early morning canoe trip just after dawn, when the lake was still and the morning mist still hovered over the water. It was a great time to think. During one of these canoe trips, it occurred to me that many of those enrolling in the *Successful Investing and Money Management* might be interested in subscribing to an investment advisory newsletter.

The *Successful Investing and Money Management* course was teaching people how to invest. It seemed logical they would also be interested in getting tips on specific investment opportunities.

On returning to the dock after my canoe trip, I was greeted by Bill Vernon, our VP Marketing and asked what he thought about this new product idea. He shared my enthusiasm, insisting we should make it the first item discussed at the meeting that was about to start. The whole group bought into the idea. On August 16, 1996 we launched *The MoneyLetter* in Canada. It was published twice a month.

It was the first and only "instant success" of my career.

The few first issue of *The MoneyLetter,* included no big name writers. The topic for each issue was selected by our editorial staff, and we retained qualified, but not big name, professionals to come with specific investment recommendations. A few months later we convinced Morty Shulman to write a regular *MoneyLetter* article, and later we added more celebrities to our list of contributors. With these celebrity writers, the circulation rose even faster.

Most of the competing investment advisories of the day were professionally designed and had the look and feel of a magazine that contained news that was probably a bit outdated by the time it was delivered to readers.

We felt *MoneyLetter* readers wanted to get "hot breaking news" on investment opportunities. To give *The MoneyLetter* the feel of "breaking news", it was designed to have the look and feel of news that was reaching readers in real time, before any time was wasted making it look good. We were not concerned about the odd typo, or designing articles to look great on the page. Our priority was simple. Our readers would be the first to get in on the hottest investment opportunities, before this news would drive prices higher. Well-meaning friends, would regularly ask why I didn't do something about the *MoneyLetter's rag-tag design.* I'd just smile and thank them for their frank comments.

The following year we began publishing editions of the *MoneyLetter* for the US market and the French language market in Canada.

We promoted *The MoneyLetter* to everyone who had enrolled in *Successful Investing and Money Management*. Within a year, we had over 100,000 subscribers.

As the company grew, we were no longer bootstrapping new product development. We recruited and trained an editorial staff in the Hume method for creating effective self-study programs using state of the art pedagogical techniques. We would invest over $1,000,000 to market test and develop new self-study and investment advisory services. These included: *The TaxLetter, The SuperInvestor Files* and *Success Over 50*.

It gave me pleasure being in the business of helping people to live better lives. Here is an example of the feedback I received from one enrollee in the *Successful Investing and Money Management program*. This story occurred when my wife and I had driven from Toronto and were spending a night at a Bed & Breakfast before catching a morning ferry to Nantucket. We checked into the Bed & Breakfast late in the afternoon, and owner offered to serve us tea and homemade scones in their library.

While waiting for our tea, my wife saw a copy of the *Successful Investing and Money Management* course on the bookshelf. When our host arrived with the tea, we asked if he had taken the course. Upon learning I was the Hume who published the course, he shook my hand vigorously and said "if it wasn't for you we wouldn't own this place."

Before buying the Bed & Breakfast, he was working at a boring job with an insurance company. For years, he and his wife had dreamed of owning their own Bed & Breakfast, but felt they would never be able to accumulate the money required to buy one. Then he enrolled in the *Successful Investing and Money Management* course. The young couple were diligent in applying what they had learned. Within five years, they were able to buy their dream Bed & Breakfast. They had taken possession earlier that year. He was so appreciative of how the course had turned their lives around that he insisted our stay was to be free of charge. I slept well that night.

Chapter 14

Marketing to the Masses

- - - - - - - -

From the day Hume Publishing was founded, my goal was to build a company providing the general public with the know-how required to manage and invest their hard earned income. Those who acquire the skills to manage and invest money live healthier, fuller, and more prosperous lives, and are more likely rètire with a comfortable nest egg. Sadly, little focus is placed on teaching money management skills in high school or advanced education curriculums.

Launching the *Successful Investing and Money Management* self-study course was the first step in realizing my dream. The next step was building a marketing organization capable of convincing tens of thousands of working people in the US and Canada to sign up for the course.

We had retained Wunderman Direct to handle the launch of the *Successful Investing and Money Management* self-study program. Now it was time to recruit a full-time marketing executive to bring the company's marketing in-house.

Bill Vernon, one of my neighbors in Markham had the ideal credentials for this assignment. All I had to do was convince him to take the job. With some not so gentle selling, Bill was recruited as Hume's Vice-president Marketing. Before joining Hume, he was a Vice-president at McLaren Advertising, managing the General Motors Canada account. Bill was a handsome man, who looked and spoke like an adverting executive who could have been perfectly cast in the TV show Mad Men. Although he had no experience in direct-to-consumer mass marketing, Bill knew the advertising business, and how to recruit and manage a big company advertising and marketing team.

With Vernon setting up our in-house marketing department, and Bill Baker in the process of building our mass marketing management software system, we were ready to sever our relationship with Wunderman Direct. We needed a team 100% dedicated to selling the *Successful Investing and Money Management* course.

We were paying Wunderman significant fees to have their staff work on the Hume Publishing account. By bringing the marketing team in-house we'd save about $7,000 per month and have direct control of our marketing program.

It was Bill Vernon's job to recruit and train the team we would need to implement the company's marketing strategy using the company's powerful mass marketing management software.

From now on all of our marketing would be handled in-house, with one exception. We would use only top-gun freelance copywriters.

Top-gun copywriters are in a league of their own. They are much like all-star athletes who regularly lead the league in home runs or goals scored. Like athletes, their skills are honed by regularly competing with other direct response copywriters in copy tests. The most successful companies selling directly to consumers routinely test two or more creative approaches before rolling out with a major direct-to-consumer marketing program.

The best direct response copywriters work on a freelance basis. Because of their proven effective ability to generate sales, they command fees that are often more than the salaries paid to the Presidents of their client companies.

- This situation makes it difficult for small companies with limited budgets to retain the services of top-gun copywriters. After becoming aware of the amazing response rates generated by these top-guns, we decided take the bull by the horns and pay whatever it cost to have them take on writing assignments for Hume Publishing. I would be thrilled if one of Hume's direct response copywriters earned more in fees that my annual salary. My big payoff would be realized by owning shares in the company. If Hume Publishing was to become a major force in direct-to-consumer mass marketing, we needed to use top-gun copywriters.

After making the decision to go after the top-gun writers Bill Vernon came up with a short list of those we would target. He was very clever in identifying the top-gun copywriters.

He did this by getting back issues of direct-response trade publications and tracking down the copywriters who were multiple award winners. We decided to approach eight of them.

Only two of the eight would consider working with a small unknown company. These were Chris Stagg who was lived in Carmel California and Hank Burnett who happened to live in Santa Barbara, about a two hour drive south of Stagg's home.

The next week Bill and I flew to San Francisco, rented a car, and headed south.

This was my first trip to California, the weather was perfect, and driving down the coastal highway was exciting. We enjoyed the ocean vistas and glorious seaside meadows of wild flowers. At one point we stopped at a beautiful lagoon and saw a group of languid sea lions sunning on the beach.

After having lunch at a café in downtown Carmel, we found our way to Chris Stagg's home. We looked forward to our first meeting with one of America's best direct response copywriters.

A brash and outgoing New Yorker in his mid-fifty's, Chis greeted us warmly and we got right down to business taking him through the *Successful Investing and Management* course. We told him of our plans to market it nationally across the US. He shared our enthusiasm for the project and agreed to write a package for us. The fee he quoted might seem outlandish to anyone that doesn't understand the mass marketing business, and why the top writers can command these fees. It was $12,000 to write a single promotion, (about $25,000 in 2021). However, if we wanted the best we'd have to pay for the best. Chris's terms were accepted.

That evening we stayed at a hotel in downtown Carmel and in the morning headed south for our meeting with Hank Burnett in Santa Barbara. This took us through Big Sur and its majestic sequoia forest.

Hank Burnet was a quiet elegant Bostonian. Like Chris Stagg Hank was in his mid-fifties but where Chris was brash and outgoing, Hank was reserved and modest. We met in the back garden of his home. To the east we could see green mountains in the distance, to the West was the Pacific Ocean shimmering in the sun. Hank quizzed us for at least two hours on the *Successful Investing and Money Management* course, and our ideas on the specific consumer groups who might be interested in taking it. Like Chis Stagg, he agreed there was probably a big US market for our course.

The meeting wrapped up with Hank agreeing to write a direct response email package for the *Successful Investing and Money Management* course. His fee was the same as that quoted by Stagg. But Hank had a backlog of work, and it would be three months before he could deliver his direct mail package.

As we learned in dealing with many of the top-gun direct response copywriters, most of them are in their fifties or older. It takes decades of experience to master the art of direct response copywriting. The best of them have this in common with top artists and musicians. They each have a distinct and easily recognizable writing style.

Now, with Chris Stagg and Hank Burnett creating the copy for our first major marketing test, all the pieces were in place to tackle the US market. We had the world's first automated mass marketing software system, and two of the world's best copywriters creating two alterative marketing strategies we would test head to head.

In consultation with Chris Stagg and Hank Burnett, we decided to use direct mail in the campaigns they were developing. It was a choice between a direct mail and a free standing insert in magazines or newspapers. We decided on direct mail because this enabled us to run more test panels than was possible testing through free standing inserts.

Our first in-house developed US direct mail tests launched about six months after that first trip to California. When the test results were in and analysed the winning package was created by Hank Burnett. This was established as the "control" against which future tests would be measured. In head-to-head competitions between copywriters the variance between the best and worst performing sales packages could range from 5% to 50%. In the competition between Hank and Chris the winning margin was about 15%.

With the successful implementation of the direct mail test we had achieved another important milestone. Now, with our powerful mass marketing software combined with ad campaigns created by the world's best direct response copywriters, sales of the *Successful Investing and Money Management* course grew exponentially in both the US and Canadian markets.

As a matter of policy 20% of our marketing budget was allocated to ongoing marketing tests. We were testing the relative effectiveness of direct mail, free standing inserts, full page ads financial publications including *The Wall Street*

Journal and *USA Today*. As well, we tested TV infomercials and radio ads.

Now, with access to many of the top-gun copywriters we set up a process we'd use on an ongoing basis to ensure we got full value from this remarkable pool of talent.

Before for setting and running major test campaigns. We would invite two or three of the top-ranked freelance copywriters to our offices in Toronto or Los Angeles for joint briefing sessions. During these briefings our marketing team would provide details on the self-study program and its features and benefits. We would discuss the enrollment fees we planned to charge, and the demographics of the consumers we felt would most benefit from buying the product or service being discussed.

At the conclusion of these briefing sessions, the competing copywriters would each head off to write a sales package accompanied by a suggested price and offer test. By getting the full creative team and the copywriters together for these briefings everyone benefited from the cross polarization of ideas.

As Hume Publishing's public profile grew, we were able to attract more elite copywriters. These included Gary Bencivenga, Stu Maltin, Gerry Schwartz, Mary Wells, and Clayton Makepeace.

We began entering our ad campaigns in the annual Canadian Direct Marketing Association competitions. We were regularly winning marketing awards such as best performing direct mail campaign, best copy, best design etc. Two years in a row we won more CDMA marketing awards than any other company in Canada including giants such as *Reader's Digest*. In 1983, I was honored by being awarded the American Marketing Association's (Toronto Chapter) Donald B. McCaskill Award for Marketing Excellence.

With our rapid growth in the US market Bill Vernon moved to Los Angeles to manage the massive US market from the front lines. Our entire management team was ecstatic at the company's rapid rate of growth. I was now splitting my time between Toronto, LA, and Atlanta. Several times a week, I'd go to the mail room to watch the arrival of hundreds of mail bags each filled with enrollments in the *Successful Investing and Money Management* course.

When in Toronto, I would meet regularly with Claudette Coburn, Hume Publishing Canada's Vice-President Marketing. We would discuss current test results, her thoughts on new marketing strategies, and she would update me on new campaigns in the pipeline. It was exciting to learn about new copywriters who had come up with breakthrough campaigns, or of a new mailing list with the potential to increase the size of our mailing universe. A classy and feisty redhead in her mid-thirties, Claudette was a gifted marketer. She played a major role in building the company's reputation as a mass marketing powerhouse. I was disappointed when left Hume to set up her own direct response marketing ad agency.

We tested a variety of media including TV infomercials, full-page ads in *US Today, The Wall Street Journal,* and *The Financial Post* in Canada, direct mail, and free standing inserts in daily newspapers. The most consistently profitable media were direct mail and free standing inserts.

Within six months of launching our national direct response program in the US, we were receiving hundreds of testimonials each month from *Successful Investing and Money Management* enrolees who had made sizable profits by applying what they learned through the course. This was pure gold for our copy writers. With this steady stream of testimonials we began publishing a quarterly eight page magazine entitled *Millionaire*. Each year over 250 million copies of *Millionaire* were delivered as free standing inserts in major newspapers and financial publications across the US and Canada.

Hume Publishing was on its way to becoming the biggest home-study company in the US and Canada. By the mid-1980s, over 250,000 Americans and Canadians were enrolling in the *Successful Investing and Money Management* course each year. As well, we extended our line of publications to include home-study programs in *Successful Real Estate Investing, Successful Small Business Management*, and *The SuperInvestor Files*, and periodicals including *The MoneyLetter* and *The TaxLetter*.

The company had over 200 employees working in three locations. Sales and publishing operations in Los Angeles and Toronto and a 30,000 square foot distribution centre in suburban Atlanta.

As I write this memoir in 2021 mass marketing tests can be carried out through electronic media in days rather than months, and at a fraction of the cost. But one thing has not changed. Regardless of the media used, the quality of the copywriting is a major factor in the success of every mass marketing campaign.

In 2019, the top-earning direct response copywriter was Clayton Makepeace. It has been reported, earned $3,000,000 that year. Sadly Clayton, who did a few jobs for Hume Publishing when he was a young man was a victim of Covid 19 and passed away in 2020.

Today top-gun freelance direct-response copywriters charge a base fee, plus a performance-based royalty. I may have been partly responsible to the introducing the practice of paying copywriters success based remuneration packages.

In the mid-1980s, one the best direct response copywriters retained by Hume Publishing was Gary Bencivenga. When we received the copy for his first direct mail campaign it included an 18-page sales letter! I called Gary complaining that no one was going to read an 18-page letter and furthermore, the cost to print and pay the postage on this monstrous package would make it unprofitable. Gary quietly listened to my whining and said, *"Who's the marketing guy, you or me? If I wasn't confident this package is a winner, I wouldn't have sent it to you."* Then he offered me this deal. If I would send out his package with the 18-page letter, he'd cut his fee in half. However, if his copy was the winner, and become the control package, we would pay him an additional $5 for every 1,000 copies of this mailing we sent out, as long as his package continued to be the control. This sales campaign was an amazing success. By the time we found a more productive direct mail package, Gary had earned almost $70,000 on that blockbuster direct mail program.

Today, direct mail is probably the most under used and underappreciated marketing media for selling products and services. When Hume Publishing used direct mail as a primary sales media, those buying a product or service had to fill out an order card by hand, and enclose it together with a check or credit card information, in a postage paid reply envelope, and walk this to the nearest post box. Despite this cumbersome order process, Hume Publishing was generating an average response rate of 1.5% on its direct mail promotions.

Today, the direct mail purchasing process is much easier and takes a fraction of the time. Buyers are directed to the seller's website where orders can be processes in a few minutes from a mobile phone.

Because it is now so much easier to respond, direct mail response rates have increased dramatically in recent years. Here are some recent statistics on direct mail marketing from *Small Business Trends, an award winning online publication.*

- ✓ Direct mail generates a motivation score that is 20% higher than digital media.
- ✓ Direct mail was found to require 21% less cognitive effort. That means the message is absorbed more quickly and effectively.
- ✓ Brand recall was 70% higher among participants who were exposed to direct mail ads rather than to digital ones.
- ✓ 62 percent of consumers who responded to direct mail in the past three months made a purchase.

Direct Mail vs. Email Statistics

- 80-90% of direct mail gets opened, only 20-30% of email gets opened on a good day.
- The response rate to direct mail pieces is 3.7%, as opposed to 2% for mobile phones, 1% email, 1% social media, and 0.2% internet display.
- 70% of consumers preferred traditional mail for receiving unsolicited offers from companies.
- When asked, "Which is more effective at getting you to take action?" 30% of millennials said direct mail, 24% said email.

A recent report from the *Direct Marketing Association* cites an average response rate to direct mail promotions at 9% in 2018, significantly up from 2017, when it was 5.1%. The prospect list response rate was 4.9%, also showing a big increase compared to the 2.9% it achieved the year before.

It seems that many of today's young marketers are asleep at the switch, assuming direct mail advertising is as irrelevant today as a slide rule or abacus. In 2020 while offering advice to two young marketers they laughed in my face when I suggested they use direct mail rather than electronic media.

The key to building long-term success when selling any product or service is establishing its credibility and quality. When the *Successful Investing and Money Management* self-study program was launched, we had no testimonials or endorsements from satisfied clients. To give the program instant credibility, we recruited an Advisory Board of high profile personalities to endorse the program.

In Canada, members of our Advisory Board included: Bill Neapole, Past President of The Royal Bank of Canada, Pierre Lortie, prominent business personality and President of The Montreal Stock Exchange, Fred McCutcheon, a past Chairman of Toronto Stock Exchange, Dr. Morton Shulman, author of the best-selling book *Anyone Can Make a Million*, and Andrew Sarlos, Chairman of Sarlos and Associates, a prominent Canadian wealth advisory service.

In the US, members of Hume Publishing's Advisory Board included Archie Roe, Chairman of Allstate Insurance, William Simone, Former Secretary of the US Treasury and Louis Rukeyser, the host of *Wall Street Week*, a top rated PBS TV show, and Kingman Doulas, a past Managing Director of Merrill Lynch. We were able to recruit this remarkable group of advisors because they believed in the need for a high quality educational program that taught money management and investing skills.

Our highest profile US advisory board member was Bill Simon, who served as Secretary of the Treasury under Presidents Nixon and Ford. When we approached Simon to join our Advisory Board he had recently achieved international notoriety by taking the Gibson greeting card company public. On an investment of $330,000, this brilliantly executed leveraged buyout netted Simon a profit of about $70 million within eighteen months. Before joining our Advisory Board he insisted on meeting with me to learn more about the *Successful Investing and Money Management* course. This presented a problem as no commercial flights would get me to Simon's Morristown New Jersey office within the time frames he was available. But Bill Simon was big catch, so I made the decision to rent a private jet for a half day in order to get Simon on board in time to be featured in our upcoming marketing program.

This was the first experience renting an executive jet and it is a highly efficient method of travel when used in coordination with a private limo for ground transportation. Within three hours of departing from Toronto I arrived at Simon's office. I was surprised to find it located in a low-rise commercial strip-mall in a rather rundown neighborhood. The wood paneled offices were far from the opulence I had expected for such a powerful man. Simon was courteous, down to earth, and exuded energy and intelligence. We got right down to business discussing the importance of the general public having access to an educational program teaching investing and money management skills. Simon was impressed with our program and agreed to join our Advisory Board. By 6:30 that evening I was at home in Toronto having dinner with my wife and kids. This was a good day's work, and the cost to rent the jet was only $6,500. It was a great investment for Hume Publishing. My kids were impressed that since seeing them off to school that morning, I had visited with a powerful man who lived in another country, and returned home in time to have dinner with them.

Each member of our Advisory Boards was paid a modest retainer. As well as the retainer, twice each year we would invite them to a weekend meeting at a luxury resort. During these weekend sessions advisory board members would review and offer advice on how our self-study programs could be improved. The business portion of the weekend was a half day meeting. The rest of the time they enjoyed hanging out together and discussing issues of the day. Today, every member of the Hume Publishing Advisory Boards would be considered a one percenter. They were NOT serving on a Hume Advisory board for the modest fees they received.

The decade before the 1987 market crash was one of the most enjoyable and fulfilling periods of my life. Over 250,000 individuals in the US and Canada were taking a Hume self-study program each year, or subscribing to one of our investment newsletters.

The success achieved by Hume Publishing was exceeding my wildest dreams. The mass marketing software we developed was a smashing success, the envy of the mass marketing industry. Much of my time was spent discussing issues and ideas with some of the best marketing minds in North America.

I was living on adrenalin. Divorced from Patricia my first wife, I had married Penny and we had a big home in a prestigious downtown Toronto neighborhood, a garden apartment in a Northern suburb of Atlanta, near or distribution center, and a condo on Wilshire Blvd in Los Angeles. The condo in LA was a short walk from both Hume Publishing's Westwood Office and the UCLA campus.

Life was flat out action. There always seemed to be another plane to catch and more to get done than there was time to do it. About every six months I would break a Toronto to LA trip with a stop off in Tucson to visit Canyon Ranch. There my batteries would be recharged by eating healthy meals at a table for one, playing tennis or hiking in the hills during the day, having a pre-dinner massage, and going to bed early. Within four or five days I was ready to climb back on the merry-go-round.

On reflection, I was probably driving myself and Hume's management team too hard. But when on a roll with an all-consuming project, I find slowing down is next to impossible.

This obsession for getting totally involved in a project may well be an incurable disorder. These days I'm waking up about four every morning, my head swimming with remembrances described in this book. This may well be a symptom of "severe entrepreneurship", if such a condition is described in the psychiatric handbook. And if it is not, maybe it should be.

Chapter 15

New Horizons

-- -- -- -- -- -- -- --

Hume Publishing's management team was doing a great job building the company's core business. Alan Booth had been wooed away from Wunderman Direct to head up Hume Publishing's operations in the US and Canada. Annual sales had broken through $40,000,000, The 2021 equivalent of almost $100,000,000. Both the US and Canadian companies were profitable and growing fast.

When stock markets were on the rise, our advertising prompted people to enroll in the *Successful Investing and Money Management* course and learn how to build their wealth by taking advantage of the raging bull market. When markets were flat or falling, our ads prompted the public to sign up for the course in order to protect their wealth and financial wellbeing.

Major ad campaigns went out twice a year, when response rates were at their peak. The effectiveness of each ad campaign was pretested a few weeks before its launch. I was proud of the world-class direct-to-consumer mass marketing capabilities we had developed.

Over the previous eighteen months, two US-based companies had expressed interest in acquiring Hume Publishing. At that time, we had no interest in selling. At the rate we were growing, it was my view the company's value would likely double or triple within the next five years.

My life was full and exciting. With the business doing well, Penny and I were taking annual biking holidays in France, visiting New York and London to take in theatre, skiing at Aspen, Mammoth, and Whistler, and holidaying on Nantucket each summer.

We spent weekends at our country home. I would play golf or tennis, and we spent time with friends and family. During the winter months, we visited with Penny's parents in Florida. Although I was still going into the office on a regular basis, the executives running Hume Publishing were doing a great job.

To this point, my entrepreneurial life had been a steady run of successes, other than the shaky US and Canadian start-ups with the *Successful Investing and Money Management* course. However, as the months rolled on I was growing restless, missing what I most enjoyed, the job of being an entrepreneur. Starting companies is my passion.

As the company's CEO, there was no specific management role for me. Having passed through the start-up phase, my entrepreneurial skills were no longer needed. Entrepreneurs who found companies do not necessarily have the ideal skill set to manage their day-to-day operations as an established business. Recognizing this, we recruited a great team of professional managers to run the day-to-day operations. But my entrepreneurial skills were not being utilized. Something had to change.

That something became clear during a holiday on Nantucket Island, where most summers we rented a beach house. It is a great place to recharge your batteries, and reflect on life.

Nantucket is an old fishing island just 14 miles long with a paved and a lightly trafficked road circumnavigating the island. It's perfect for biking. Before breakfast each morning, I would get on my bike and do a circuit of the island. From every vantage point along the route you can enjoy ever changing seascapes. You ride past unsettled seaside moors, then rose-covered fishing huts clad in weathered grey shingles with bright blue hydrangea dotting the front gardens. For me, biking is the ideal way to think clearly and sort out issues.

While relaxing into the first bike ride of my holiday, with the wind in my hair and enjoying the rhythm of biking, the reason for my restlessness became crystal clear. My business life had become boring.

Starting companies is my passion, but now Hume Publishing had evolved through its entrepreneurial stage. Now I was a spectator watching from the sidelines. It was time to set off on a new entrepreneurial adventure.

Upon returning from the Nantucket holiday, a meeting of the Hume Publishing Board was arranged to discuss my role in the company. This proposal was tabled: Beginning immediately, I would take on a new responsibility as the manager of new Business Development. My time would be devoted to growing The Hume Group of Companies both horizontally and vertically, following the McGraw Hill model. The board was onside with this. It was agreed that I would move into a new office in Toronto's business district, away from the publishing company.

During my first week as Hume Publishing's Director of Business Development, we came up with a short list of projects to be perused. We would explore non-publishing opportunities in the field of investing and money management and examine publishing opportunities outside the fields of investing and money management. Having set these parameters, the first project to be pursued was obvious.

We would set up a mutual fund company. Every year we were receiving hundreds of inquiries from those enrolled in the *Successful Investing and Money Management* course asking if our investment experts would manage their money. Many people don't have the time or inclination to be their own wealth manager. The obvious response to this demand was to set up our own mutual funds. This was the first proposal coming from Hume's new Business Development unit. It was immediately approved by the board.

When the decision was made to found The Hume Group of Funds, we re-organized the corporate structure. Both Hume Publishing and The Hume Group of Funds were set up as separate business units of The Hume Group of Companies.

Within this new corporate structure, we explored publishing opportunities in the health-care sector. It seemed likely Hume's expertise in teaching people investing and money management skills could be applied to keeping them healthy.

For expert advice on unmet consumer health-care needs, a meeting was arranged with Dr. John Evans, the founding Dean of McMaster University's Medical School. We met for lunch at Toronto's King Edward hotel. At the time, the internet was a new phenomenon, and we had no idea how this development was to turn the publishing industry on its head.

Dr. Evans wasted no time in identifying a significant unmet need in the health care sector. He suggested we develop a series of patient-education programs for those with chronic medical conditions. Learning how to manage chromic conditions on a day-to-day basis is critical to achieving optimum outcomes, but in general practice, doctors do not have the time to provide this training. Dr. Evans suggested we start by developing programs for those with angina and heart disease, high blood pressure, migraine headache, diabetes, arthritis, and asthma.

Over lunch, we did some brainstorming on a format for delivering this patient education and how to make it easily available to the general public. After an hour or so of exchanging ideas, here's what we came up with: The patient education would be delivered through an attractively packaged multi-media package that included a video and printed training manual. These would be distributed through major drugstore chains in the US and Canada. To make it easy for pharmacists to refer Hume's patient-education programs, they would be displayed in attractive kiosks placed in the drugstore's pharmacy section.

At the end of a much longer than expected lunch, we were all enthused about this heath care business opportunity. Dr. Evans expressed interest in making an investment in this new venture. I was too, if this was necessary to get the business underway as soon as possible.

At our next board meeting, this patient-education publishing opportunity was presented as a future business opportunity. Although there was unanimous agreement on the merits of the project, it was clear the company could not simultaneously fund both a new mutual fund company and a large-scale medical publishing project.

Some board members suggested moving ahead with the medical publishing project with the initial funding coming from outside investors. Later, when the mutual-fund company was successfully launched, The Hume Group of Companies would acquire a major equity position in the medical publishing project.

With the approval of The Hume Group's board, Dr. John Evans, myself, and one of our board members, agreed to invest $300,000 to establish a new patient-education healthcare publishing company.

With this funding in place, my wife Penny was recruited to manage the product development. As a certified gerontologist with publishing experience, she was well qualified to take on this project. As well, Penny's visual design talents would ensure our educational videos were engaging to a general audience. Based on her success in developing Hume Publishing's *Success over 50* program, we knew she was up to the challenge.

The next step was to run a small test of the patient education concept. This was an essential first step before major funding was arranged to develop and market a full range of patient education programs. The test involved producing a single book-video package on how to manage chronic asthma. It was released under the brand name "HUMED". For our marketing test, the asthma patient education program was packaged in a six unit counter display, and placed in the pharmacy section of 100 Canadian pharmacies. This test was taking place during same time period as The Hume Group of Funds was being set up.

Sales of the asthma patient education program met our objectives over a four-month test period in Canadian drugstores. With the completion of a successful marketing test, the decision was made to raise $4,000,000 and develop a line of six patient education programs. These would be distributed through major drugstore chains across the US and Canada.

Developing patient education programs on chronic disease management was especially important to me as I had been living with chronic asthma for years. Every spring with the budding of new leaves, I would have an outbreak of asthma, as well attacks would be triggered by extremely cold winter weather. Many times I had to stop playing tennis or skiing because of an asthma attack. A holiday trip to Trinidad had to be cut short because of a severe asthma attack induced by visiting a wild animal preserve.

The medical consultant Dr. Evan's recruited for our asthma patient education program was Dr. Fredrick Hargreave, Professor of Medicine at McMaster University. At the time, he was considered one of the world's leading authorities on the treatment of asthma. During my first conversation with Hargreave, my issues with chronic asthma came up. He said, "Ron, we can get your asthma under control right now, if you will give me your undivided attention for fifteen minutes. But you must agree to follow my instructions every day of your life, whether or not, you are having asthma symptoms." After my lifelong battle with asthma, I was skeptical, but agreed to follow Dr. Hargrave's instructions to the letter. Since that amazing day, I have never suffered a major asthma attack, regardless of the pollen count, the weather, or when playing tennis or skiing. For me, this patient education venture was already a life-changing event, and we had not yet released a single new product.

To head up the HUMED Company, we recruited an American who had previously worked as the National Sales Manager for a major US cosmetics company, and for several years had held a senior management position with Revlon Canada. He was an authority on marketing products through drugstore chains in both the US and Canada. Because I have not been able to track him down and get his OK to be named in this book, I'll refer to him as John M.

With John M on board, we development a detailed business plan for HUMED. Our financial forecasts indicated that it would require an investment of $4,000,000 to fund the company start up. One of the first venture-capital companies we met with was interested in providing the entire amount we were raising, subject to their usual due diligences. They were impressed that HUMED's founding shareholders had funded a successful marketing test. They liked the fact that Dr. John Evans was advising on our product development, and was in the process of recruiting a blue-chip Medical Advisory Board to give the patient education line instant credibility. We were impressed by their knowledge of the North American drugstore industry. As well, we got along well with their financing team. It felt like an ideal fit. John M and I high-fived each other as we headed for the elevator after our successful meeting with the venture capital company.

A day after arriving back in Toronto, a friend called to let me know *Canadian Business* magazine had done a cover story on Hume Publishing. The article was entitled "Hard Times at the House of Hume." This was not good news. The article was written by the friend of a disgruntled employee who had recently been fired from a senior management role at Hume Publishing. In an act of vengeance, he provided fictitious and misleading information on Hume's operations and suggested the company was squandering vast amounts of money on out-of-town management meetings.

When the *Canadian Business* article came to our attention, it had to be disclosed to the New York venture capital company.

They thanked us for disclosing the article, but the damage was done. Their offer to fund the company was withdrawn.

It was back to square one on the funding issue. This was going to be tough in light of the *Canadian Business* article. It was time to be innovative. We would continue to pursue other venture capital companies, and we would also try another approach.

We planned to look for a strategic investor. If HUMED was a success, the company would need a printer to manufacture hundreds of thousands of books. This would be an attractive contract for any book printer. We did some research and came up with a list of about twenty privately-owned printing companies in the US and Canada with the capabilities of manufacturing the books HUMED planned to publish. Most were in mid-America states, including Oklahoma, Iowa, Wisconsin, and Illinois. As well, two were in Ontario, Canada.

Then, we arranged a series of twelve meetings with the owners of these printing companies. We made each of them this offer. If they would invest a minimum of $500,000 in HUMED, on the same terms offered to the venture capital companies, their company would be awarded the contract to print our line of patient-education manuals, as long as their pricing and quality was within 2% of the price quoted by competitive printers.

By accepting this deal, the printing company owner had a double-edged opportunity. Their printing company would have a major new client, and assuming HUMED's success, the owner would make a substantial capital gain. Several of the printing company owners were interested, and the first to accept was based in suburban Toronto.

In the meantime, we were still pursuing venture-capital companies in the US and Canada. With this two-pronged financing strategy, it took about six months to raise the required funding through a syndicate of private investors led by a Chicago-based venture-capital company and the Toronto-based printer.

With the funding in place, Dr. Evans recruited a team of leading doctors to serve as HUMED's International Advisory Board on Patient Education. The doctors on this Advisory Board were prominently featured on the packaging of our patient education programs and on all advertising and promotional materials. Members of this advisory board included: Dr. John Evans, Dr. Norman Kaplan, Head of the Hypertension Section at the University of Texas, Dr. E, William Hancock, Stanford University Medical School, Dr. Mayer Davidson, UCLA Medical School, and Dr. John Mills, Director of the Arthritis/Rheumatism Clinic at Massachusetts General Hospital.

After the damaging article on Hume Publishing was published, we launched a libel action against *Canadian Business*. At that time, they were owned by Rogers Communications. The case was settled almost a year later with *Canadian Business* admitting their culpability and agreeing to pay a negotiated settlement. This situation was especially troubling as I had a friendly longstanding relationship with Jim Warrillow, the publisher of *Canadian Business*. I knew him to be a gentleman. As soon as the matter was settled, Warrillow invited me to his office to pick up the settlement check. Upon arriving for our meeting, John Tory, at that time the CEO of Rogers, joined us. Both Warrillow and Tory wanted to apologize for the libelous article. This gesture was much appreciated. Warrilow said he wanted to apologize as soon as he learned about the article, but was advised by their lawyer not to contact me until the legal issue was settled. Shortly after our meeting, Tory resigned from Rogers Communications and is now the Mayor of Toronto.

When the **HU**MED patient education programs were officially launched, John M had successfully sold the line into every major drugstore chain in the US including Walgreen, RightAid and CVS, and in Canada, London Drugs and Shopper's Drug Mart agreed to carry the line. Our patient education packages were displayed in attractive kiosks placed strategically near each store's pharmacy section.

For the first two years after their launch, the **HU**MED patient education programs easily met the revenue per square feet criteria required by the drug store chains, and a number of drugstores carrying the line steadily increased. Then, despite our efforts to support sales through advertising and in drugstore flyers, the sales per square foot began to gradually drop-off in every chain carrying the line.

As the declining sales continued, it became clear the Internet was changing the world forever. Now consumers could get quality patient education free of charge without leaving home by visiting websites operated by Harvard Medical School, The Mayo Clinic, and WebMD. As the pace of declining sales accelerated, the **HU**MED line was being dropped as it was no longer meeting the drugstore chain's revenue per square foot requirements. With no alternative distribution channels, **HU**MED was in serious trouble. We were fast running out of capital and without a proven effective distribution channel, new funding could not be raised. There was no option, but to declare bankruptcy and wind up the company.

This was my first major business failure and a bitter disappointment for me, Dr. John Evans, and the entire team that had worked so hard to develop a superb series of patient-education programs. But, as an entrepreneur, you must accept failures from time to time.

Despite this sad ending, it is my hope that the thousands of chronic disorder sufferers who purchased a **HU**med patient-education program achieved the same level success in managing their condition as I did in controlling my asthma.

Chapter 16

Hume Group of Mutual Funds

Over the years, we had countless requests from our clients – especially enrollees in the *Successful Investing and Money management* course – to have Hume manage their personal investments. Even with the wealth building tools we provided, many people did not have the time or inclination to manage their personal investment portfolio.

It was now time to give our clients what they wanted. The Hume Group would launch a mutual fund company. This was a major departure from publishing, but the demand for this service was obvious, based on the feedback received from many of the five million enrollees in the *Successful Investing and Money Management* course. This was a logical extension of our core business. The plan was to establish a successful Canadian mutual fund business, and then roll out into the US market within two years of the Canadian launch.

The future prospects for The Hume Group of Companies was exciting, assuming we had a successful launch of the Hume Funds in Canada. The Hume Group of Funds was founded in Canada in 1985. Hume Publishing invested about $2,000,000 of its retained earnings to set up the company. As well, an equal amount was raised from a Toronto-based consortium of private investors. The next step was to recruit a team of highly skilled professionals to manage the administrative side of the business.

To head up the new company, we recruited Bob Hamilton, a senior Toronto lawyer who specialized in business and finance. We had a long relationship with Bob as he was the lead lawyer on the Hume Account at Tory, Tory, Deslauriers and Bennington. Bob was in his mid-forties smart, charming, and well organized. He also knew most of the big players in Toronto's financial community. This would be important when we were launching a new financial services company.

There was much to do. We needed to establish a marketing strategy that would provide The Hume Group of Funds with a clear-cut advantage over our competitors that were well-established and well-heeled major banks and stock brokers. We were about to start doing business in the big leagues, competing against financial institutions that were household names.

Research on competing funds revealed an interesting phenomenon. Our competitors made no effort to promote the personality or public profile of their fund managers. For the most part they were faceless grey bureaucrats.

We would take advantage of this weakness by recruiting an all-star fund management team for the Hume Group of Funds. This would be the Canadian equivalent of having our funds managed by a team of several Warren Buffets. This would clearly differentiate The Hume Group of funds from our competitors. We felt this strategy would motivate investors in the bank and stockbroker-controlled funds to transfer their money to a Hume Fund.

We also planned to re-write the rule book on how mutual funds were marketed in Canada. Prior to the launch of The Hume Funds, consumers invested in mutual funds through their bank, trust company, or stockbroker. Hume was the first Canadian mutual fund company to use a mass marketing direct-to-consumer marketing strategy.

Senior executives and media pundits in the established financial community were openly critical of Hume's direct-to-consumer marketing approach. They claimed consumers needed the guidance of a professional money manager to make sound investment decisions. We vehemently disagreed with this objection. This argument did not hold water given that the professional money managers employed by banks and stock brokers were anything but objective. They were being paid to promote the Funds operated by their employer.

The powerhouse fund managers we recruited included Fredrik Y. McCutcheon, a former Chairman of The Toronto Stock Exchange and President of Arachnae Investments, Dr. Morton Shulman a successful investor and the author of two best-selling books on investing, Andrew Sarlos, Chairman of Sarlos Zuckeman renowned investment counselors, and Norman Short, President and Chairman of Guardian Capital Group, a firm that managed over $1 billion in investments. Shulman and Sarlos were also members of Hume Publishing's Advisory Board. As well as managing our client's investments, this remarkable team would keep investors in The Hume Group of Funds informed of the rationale behind their investment decisions. This all-star fund management team was front and center in all ads and promotions for The Hume Group of Funds.

To invest in a Hume Fund, consumers did not have to visit their bank or stockbroker. They simply filled out the forms included in a direct mail package that we sent to their home address. The subscription forms, and checks for the money to be invested, could be returned in a postage-paid envelope.

To test the effectiveness of our marketing strategy, we used our top-gun copywriters to create two packages that would be tested with segments of Hume Publishing clients and subscribers to various business and investment publications. Utilizing the mass marketing expertise employed so successfully by Hume Publishing, we were ready to create a new kind of Mutual Fund Company.

The effectiveness of this marketing strategy exceeded our most optimistic forecasts. In their first year, The Hume Funds attracted over $150 million in assets, and the funds' performance was amongst the best in Canada, outperforming all major stock indices. Within eighteen months of its launch, over 40,000 Canadians had invested over $250 million in The Hume Group of Funds. The Hume Group of Funds was a marketing home run.

Every business day, we would receive several large postage bags filled with subscription forms to invest in a Hume Fund. Each included a check for the funds to be invested, most for amounts ranging from $10,000 to $50,000. It was an interesting experience to visit the mail room.

We were assuming an awesome responsibility. We had to do a superb job for those who entrusted their financial wellbeing to a Hume Fund. With the effectiveness of our marketing strategy confirmed, The Hume Group of Fund, grew exponentially in sync with consumer awareness of the funds.

Our fund managers, Fred McCutcheon, Andy Sarlos, and Norman Short met for breakfast each Tuesday at 8:00 AM in the dining room of Shulman's home. Although not involved in investment decisions, I attended every fund management meeting. No one chaired them. The group worked as a highly efficient unit in discussing how best to allocate and invest the growing pot of money entrusted to our care. Each manager assumed responsibility for one sector including high quality stocks, and high yielding government and corporate bonds. The fund managers had the freedom to invest in stocks and bonds traded on exchanges across the world. Our objective was to provide the highest possible return while preserving the investor's capital.

At the beginning of each meeting, the Fund Managers were brought up to date on the amount of new money flowing into the funds over the previous week. Each fund's performance was then reviewed. The group discussed portfolio tweaks based on recent news, and made decisions on where to invest the new capital flowing into the funds.

As money being invested in the funds grew each week, the investment process became more challenging. For instance, in the early days of the Funds, the managers typically invested $50,000 in a single stock. This had little impact on the share price. However, as the funds grew, and we were investing $250,000 or more in a single stock, this increased demand drove up share prices. It was fascinating to see these incredibly talented fund managers in action.

Automated trading has dramatically changed the nature of the investing industry since the Hume Group of Funds was launched in 1985. To a large extent, this replaced the experience and creativity in the management of mutual funds.

Founding The Hume Group of Funds was one of the most rewarding periods of my entrepreneurial life. With their amazing success in Canada, we were excited about the opportunity to launch a US fund company.

Sadly, with the 1987 market crash we had no option but to sell The Hume Group of Funds. The Montreal Group that acquired The Hume Funds renamed them Altamira, now one of Canada's largest fund companies with assets exceeding $1.3 billion.

As an entrepreneur, you sometimes live on a knife edge. Had the 1987 market crash occurred two years later when The Hume Group of Funds was well established, Hume could now be a major player in the North American financial community, and I would probably be a one percenter. In the past 100 years there have been only 5 major stock market crashes in North America. We had the misfortune to launch The Hume Group of Funds during one of these periods.

But I can't complain. For over 50 years, I dodged bullets and enjoyed a long run of successes. The odds catch up with everyone over a lifetime. I had a great run and have ended my career as a happy man.

In the final analysis life is not measures by the riches you accumulate, all that really counts is the pleasure, happiness and fulfillment you've enjoyed throughout your life journey.

PART 4

SETBACKS AND RECOVERY

Chapter 17

A Tsunami strikes

In the September/October period of each year, Hume Publishing launched a massive direct-response sales campaign to generate new enrollments in the *Successful Investing and Money Management* program.

Before each major sales campaign, we pre-tested two creative themes to determine which would generate the highest response rate in the current economic environment. In 1987, these tests were conducted in late August and early September.

The winning creative theme for the autumn of 1987 roll-out was "Don't be left behind, learn how to cash in on today's raging bull market by signing up for the *Successful Investing and Money Management* course."

The Hume Group of Funds, launched the previous year, was off to a fast start. By October of 1987, over 40,000-unit holders had invested in a Hume Fund. This represented about $400,000,000 in assets under management. In the fall of 1987, The Hume Group of Funds launched a major direct mail marketing campaign. Most of these mailings were arriving in homes during the second half of October.

The Hume Group of companies was on a roll. Both the publishing company and the mutual fund company were looking forward to best-ever years.

Then a tsunamic struck.

On October 19, 1987, the stock market collapsed. The Dow plunged an astonishing 22.6%, the biggest one-day percentage loss in history, even bigger than the 1929 stock market crash, just before the Great Depression.

With this development, response rates for Hume Publishing's October sales campaign for the *Successful Investing and Money Management* course came in at less than 25% of budget. Income fell short of budget by 75%. This disappointing result occurred at a time when the company's cash reserves were low because of the funds invested in 1985 to found The Hume Group of Funds.

With the market crash, new unit holders in The Hume Group of Funds dried up overnight. Fund management revenues declined by almost 25%. At this point, the Hume Group of Funds was operating at a monthly cash flow deficit as all unit holders had come on board over the past eighteen months. We were not yet collecting sufficient income to cover the front-loaded marketing costs we had invested to generate new clients.

The Hume Group of Companies was in a serious and unanticipated cash flow bind. We needed to raise capital within the next month to meet the payroll for 200 employees, pay the outstanding amounts owing on our marketing campaigns, and cover the capitalization requirements for mutual fund companies.

To deal with the crisis, an emergency meeting of the Hume Group of Companies board of directors was arranged for the last Tuesday in October of 1987. Two separate issues had to be dealt with: The publishing company and the mutual fund company. Our CFO estimated it would take about $2,000,000 to get the publishing company back on track. Board members were confident this could be arranged within a month or so based on the company's pre-market crash track record.

It was a different situation with The Hume Group of Funds. We had no track record in the financial services industry. It would take years for the industry to recover. After a lengthy discussion, the board concluded the most prudent course of action was to sell the company. To start the ball rolling, the management team would start putting together an information package for prospective buyers.

Several well-established financial service companies expressed interest in acquiring The Hume Group of Funds. Within a few months, an agreement was reached with a Montreal-based group to acquire The Hume Group of Funds. Considering the market uncertainties after the market crash, this was a good deal for both parties. We felt comfortable the new owners had the investment management capabilities and financial resources to protect the interests of the Hume Fund unit holders. When the sale closed, the new owners dropped "The Hume Funds" name and re-branded the funds as "Altamira".

In dealing with Hume Publishing it was a different story. Over the years, many people have asked me "whatever became of Hume Publishing, the *Successful Investing and Money Management* course and *The MoneyLetter*." During the 1970s and 1980s all were well known brands in both the US and Canada.

The demise of these once thriving publications was a by-product of the 1987 stock market crash, compounded by the self-serving and unscrupulous actions of one man. He will be referred to as "TBG" (The bad guy).

After the 1987 market crash, when the decision was made to raise $2,000,000 in new capital for Hume Publishing, TBG, who was a board member, made a proposal that would solve the cash flow issue without having to raise capital from outside sources. He offered to invest $2 million in Hume Publishing by buying newly issued shares in the company. He proposed a share price that reflected the current market conditions. It was a tough deal for the company, but not unreasonable in the circumstances. After some discussion, the board accepted TBG's offer. We agreed to close on the share sale the following week.

When the follow-up meeting convened to close on the sale of shares to TBG, he did not show up. Instead, he sent his accountant with a message to the board. TBG would make the $2,000,000 investment in Hume Publishing shares, however, he had second thoughts on the share price. He wanted double the number of shares agreed to at the previous meeting.

The board members were enraged, and the company was in an impossible position. There was insufficient time to find an alternative investor before the company was insolvent. Because there was no alternative, the board reluctantly accepted TBG's terms. There was no other option.

After graduating with a law degree, TBG was recruited by a leading Toronto law firm specializing in business law. He was introduced to me through a friend when I was with McGraw Hill, Canada. I needed a corporate lawyer to assist me in making an offer to purchase McClelland and Stewart, a leading Canadian book publisher. At the time, it was rumored that Jack McClelland, the company's owner, was interested in selling out.

TBG knew the legal costs were a stretch for me. To help me out, he agreed to prepare an offer to purchase McClelland and Stewart and bill me at his going rate, but not send me the invoice until after a deal was closed. Instead, he proposed this quid pro quo. TBG would become the lawyer of record for McClelland and Stewart if the proposed deal went through and, if we failed to acquire McClelland and Stewart, TBG would be retained to act as the lawyer for any subsequent business I founded. As it turned out, Jack McClelland decided not to sell the company.

In accordance with our deal, when Hume Publishing was founded, TBG was appointed as the company's lawyer. He made an investment in shares of Hume Publishing and joined the company's board of directors.

By the early 1980's, before the launch of The Hume Group of Funds, Hume Publishing was doing well in both the US and Canada. With this success, we were on the radar screen of a New York-based mergers and acquisition company specializing in publishing and media companies. They initiated talks to see if we might be open to an acquisition.

For me, this was an interesting opportunity that had to be taken seriously. Through the sale of Hume Publishing, I would make a substantial capital gain, and the buyers would likely retain me to continue running the company. On the other hand, selling the company at this point would cap the upside for other investors in the company. In discussing this with TBG, we both agreed the company's value would likely double over the next few years if our growth trajectory was maintained. For this reason, we declined to proceed with discussions on selling Hume Publishing at that time.

TBG suggested that, if I wanted to take some money out of Hume, he would purchase a portion of my shares for $1,000,000, about $2,000,000 in 2021. I agreed, subject to one condition. I did not want to lose control of the company and, by accepting TBG's offer, I would no longer be the company's biggest shareholder. To put me at ease on this issue, TBG suggested that an agreement be set up so that I had the right to continue as Hume Publishing's CEO if my ownership stake in the company was at least 15%. With this condition agreed to, we closed on the deal.

In the meantime, TBG's career continued to skyrocket. He became a partner at his law firm at an early age. A few years later, TBG was recruited as CEO of a major international resource company and was appointed to the Senate of Canada.

One day, he called and asked to speak with me on a highly confidential personal matter. Turns out he was having an affair and claimed to have fallen in love with a legal secretary at his firm. This was awkward as he had a wife and five children. TBG felt it would be easier for him to carry on the affair if his mistress did not work at the law firm where he was a senior partner. Could we find a position for his mistress at Hume Publishing? With some reluctance, I agreed to give her a job. Within weeks, she confided to her colleagues at Hume about her relationship with TBG.

The situation became even more uncomfortable when TBG began bringing his mistress to Hume Publishing's out-of-town meetings with the company's management and the US and Canadian Boards of Advisors. I had met TBG's wife several times and had no appetite for acting as a co-conspirator to his infidelity. This was awkward for me and my wife Penny. We were invited to attend the marriage of TBG's daughter, and a few weeks later we were invited to dinner at the home of his mistress. On one occasion in addressing TBG's wife, I inadvertently used the mistress's name. Happily, she did not notice this slip, but my wife did.

A few months later, TBG bought his mistress a new home. It was located within a twenty minute drive from the home he shared with his wife and children. After moving into her new home, TBG's second lady arranged a housewarming party to which Penny and I were invited. At the housewarming, we were surprised to find that we were the only attendees from TBG's circle of business associates and friends. All other guests were friends and relatives of his mistress. The mistress's father, who was introduced to me by TBG, took me aside and asked if I felt TBG would ever leave his wife. TBG had introduced me to the father as a close friend. But I was not a friend, we were simply business associates. Obviously, TBG had no qualms about deceiving those he claimed to love.

This situation should have been a warning to me. If a TBG was capable of cheating on his wife so blatantly, and lying to his mistress so openly, I should have known he was not to be trusted in his dealings with me. Unfortunately, I ignored this situation. This naivety on my part was a costly mistake.

When TBG demanded double the shares agreed *to* for his $2,000,000 investment in Hume Publishing, my equity in the company fell to slightly less than 15%. In the heat of the moment, I had overlooked the full implications TBG's demands. Clearly, this had not escaped TBG's attention. When TBG received the share certificates confirming he had control of Hume Publishing, he dispatched one of his minions to inform me I was fired as the company's CEO.

TBG did not have the courage, or common courtesy, to advise me of the dismissal face-to-face. And this man was appointed to the Senate of Canada! Makes you wonder about the vetting process The Government of Canada uses to vet senators.

Had I remained in control of Hume Publishing after the crash, we would have focused on rebuilding the company as the North American market leader in providing personal investing and money management self-study programs and investment advisory services.

But, to execute his plan for Hume Publishing, TBG knew I had to go. There is no way I would have agreed to the self-serving strategy he had concocted. It was TBG's plan to groom the company for a quick sale. If successful with this strategy TBG would have realized a ten times return on the $3,000,000 he had invested in the company.

To implement his plan, TBG appointed a marketing professional to run Hume Publishing's day-to-day operations. Neither TBG nor the newly appointed President had any experience in running a publishing company. Overheads were slashed to the bare minimum by eliminating all new product development costs, cutting back on student services, disbanding the advisory boards, and selling off key assets including the company's proprietary mass marketing software.

As it turned out, TBG's plan for a quick sale of Hume Publishing at a premium price did not work out as planned. By gutting the company's core operations, the *Successful Investing and Money Management* courses quickly became outdated. This caused the dropout rate to increase dramatically, from 20% when TBG gained control of the company, to almost 40% over the next four years. Profits were plummeting. The business was going in the wrong direction, and fast.

By 1997, TBG realized his plan for a fast sale of Hume Publishing at its pre-market crash valuation had failed. At this point, he was forced to put Hume Publishing on the market at a fire-sale price. Shortly thereafter, the Company was sold to AMA, a Chicago-based company, for $19,200,000.

The day after acquiring Hume Publishing, AMA's President called me. As the company's founder, he wanted to retain me to review its current status. This offer was accepted. A review of the company's most recent monthly reports was shocking. I learned the full extent of TBG's gutting of the company's editorial and client services. This made it clear why dropout rates from the *Successful Investing and Money Management* program were escalating monthly. The company was on a downward death spiral. I was stunned to learn the company's proprietary marketing software and distribution facilities had been sold off and that TBG was draining capital from the company by paying himself almost $1,000,000 in consulting fees.

When I last met with the AMA management team, they were seriously considering a legal action against TBG for grossly understating the drop-out rate of clients who had enrolled in the *Successful Investing and Money Management* course.

After the sale of Hume Publishing, TBG devised a plan where he would not have to share the proceeds of the sale with me or other minority shareholders. When Hume Publishing was sold in 1998, TBG sent an offer to purchase my shares in the company for $18.00! Based on the number of shares I owned, and the $19,200,000 AMA paid to acquire Hume Publishing, I was expecting to receive approximately $3,000,000.

I was gob smacked, as were other minority shareholders. These included members of my family, close friends, and some of the company's senior executives and suppliers. In my view,

TBG's claim that Hume Publishing shares were worthless was a clear case of fraud. To recover our share fair share of proceeds from the sale of Hume Publishing, myself and other minority shareholders decided to launch a legal action against TBG.

To begin the process, we retained a law professor at the University of Toronto to get his opinion on the merits of our case. After reviewing the company's most recent financial statements and share ownership records, it was his assessment that our case against TBG was a slam dunk. He also warned us it would take years to wend its way through the courts, and I should budget to spend about $500,000 for my share of the legal fees. He also recommended that, because of TBG's high profile and access to top legal talent, me and my fellow litigants should recruit one of Canada's top corporate lawyers to represent us.

This was easier said than done as most of Toronto's big name corporate lawyers did work for TBG's business interests and declined to take our case. Eventually, a leading Montreal-based law firm agreed to represent us in a legal action against TBG.

My share of the initial retainer equaled about six months of my salary as The Hume Groups CEO. Our lawyer began by advising me that we would also have to retain an independent business evaluator, and considering our adversary, it was recommended we retain one of the best in the business. This was an additional retainer that could not be handled from petty cash.

The first step in pursuing the legal action was requisitioning Hume Publishing's current financial records. Because Hume Publishing was headquartered in Toronto, and the company's CFO was based there, it was reasonable to assume the company's financial records were kept in Toronto. TBG's lawyer agreed to provide access to the records, but there was a hitch. We were informed the records were spread between Toronto, Atlanta, and Los Angeles. Therefore, to complete their audit, our business valuation team would have to travel to Atlanta and Los Angeles. This increased the costs and delayed the auditing process.

TBG did everything possible to delay and increase the legal costs we were incurring. During a six-month period, my personal costs were running well over the amount I had budgeted, and the case was not close to reaching the courts. Working on the case was pretty much a full-time job.

My family became deeply concerned because of the pressure I was under. Money was flowing out, nothing was coming in. There was no end in sight for the legal action. Getting up every morning, there was only one item on my to-do list. Spending another day dealing with lawyers and business valuators. This was no way to live life.

After almost a year of being consumed by the legal action, the relationship with my wife Penny was becoming increasingly strained. We took a weekend trip to Algonquin Park to see if this would help us get back on track. The first morning, I took an early morning canoe trip. The day was perfect. The water was still. You could see a reverse image of the opposite shore mirrored in the water. For the first time in over a year, I felt a sense of peace being away from the city and away from lawyers.

As my canoe cruised silently through the still water, it became crystal clear my life was out of control and had to change. Upon returning from that morning on the water, I made the decision to drop the lawsuit.

With a new clarity of mind, I realized life is too precious to spend several years dealing with the stress, emotional drain, and the financial costs involved in pursuing the legal action against TBG. All I had to gain was money, but money alone does not buy happiness and fulfilment. My family supported this decision.

I did not know exactly what was to come next.

The five-year period following October 17, 1987 was certainly my life's most challenging time. The company I had spent almost twenty years building was gone. As well, my marriage of eighteen years with Penny was in the process of breaking up. The cost to pursue a legal action against TBG had eaten up much of my net worth. As well, legal fees were being paid to a divorce lawyer and a property settlement was being negotiated. To make matters worse two close friends, Don McGregor, and Sol Bienstock were dying of cancer.

It was time to regain control of my life. But where to begin?

I decided to work with a psychologist for guidance on how best to move forward. She suggested dealing first with the disintegrating relationship with Penny. After talking this out, I came to the realization that if Penny and I were right for one another, the marriage would have survived both the good and bad times. Penny is a good person with many fine qualities, but we are quite different people.

With Penny and I having made the decision to go our separate ways, it was time to move on with life. It took months to realize my identity was not tied to the success or failure of Hume Publishing. No matter who you are or what you do, sometimes bad things happen. Although I would never cash in on a $25 million payout, that did not mean fulfilment and happiness were impossible to achieve.

My career at McGraw Hill and in building The Hume Group of Companies was a great ride, reaching heights I could not have imagined when Hume Publishing was founded. For almost 30 years, I had enjoyed a steady run of successes with only a few minor setbacks along the way.

It was time to accept that over the spectrum of everyone's life there will be ups and downs.

About this time, Peter Copland and his wife Marilyn invited me to join them for a two-week holiday on a yacht that Marilyn had recently purchased. Starting in Victoria, we would head north for a week visiting Salt Spring Island and exploring fiords up Canada's beautiful west coast rain forests before returning to Victoria. This was a much-needed break. Hanging out with Peter and Marilyn in the peace and beauty of this sea voyage helped me in reaching a decision on how to move forward with my business life.

During a restaurant breakfast before heading back to Toronto, Peter looked me in the eye and said, "call me if you need money, it's sunny on my side of the street." My eyes teared up. I was not alone. During the plane ride back to Toronto, the realization dawned on me that, for the first time since my businesses went down in flames, I was thinking clearly.

There were many important positives in my life. My children Charron and Peter and my stepchildren Jay and Amanda, were doing well. All of them had developed successful careers and were living fulfilling lives. Charron was living in Vancouver and was a much sought-after wardrobe manager. She has worked on major movies and TV series including *Battleship Galactic* and *Once Upon a Life*. Peter was living in Los Angeles and was a successful TV writer/producer. He was the Executive Producer for *Flash Gordon* and the *Ties That Bind* series. Jay had given up a career in law and moved to LA where he had achieved success as a writer and stand-up comedian. Amanda had moved to British Columbia where she was pursuing a career in teaching. Happily, all of them have done well in life despite having a parent who focused more on business than spending time with his kids

Physically my health was good, and my confidence was returning. It was time to start on a new career path doing the work I enjoyed.

After returning from my west coast holiday, I met with the owner of a Toronto-based ad agency, and we agreed join forces in a new business where I would provide a marketing service to his agencies' advertising clients. This was a good starting point for me to re-enter the business world. This arrangement provided me with an office to work from, colleagues to work with, and a steady income.

Through the experience with TBG, I learned two vitally important lessons.

- When it becomes obvious someone is less than honest and open in any of their relationships, business or personal, move on and sever all business connections.
- When money starts flowing in from your business, resist spending your money on new toys and an expensive lifestyle. Instead, make it your #1 priority to establish an emergency fund of liquid assets in the event you run into unexpected business reversals. The size of an emergency fund should reflect the size of your business. Had I been wise enough to set up an emergency fund with the first million I took out of Hume Publishing, I would have had the financial resources to retain control of company after the market crash.

Chapter 18

Slowly, the Sun Breaks Though Again

- - - - - - - - -

Moon on bright water, shattered abruptly by stone,
Reassembles slowly

This wonderful haiku by the poet Barbara Bury sums up the period following the loss of my business empire and the breakup of my marriage to Penny.

A memoir means thinking back. It took over fifteen years to figure out what caused my world to collapse and make the changes that have enabled me to arrive at what is now my most satisfying stage of my life.

During the first three years after losing control of The Hume Group of Companies I was living in a state of shock, incapable of thinking clearly. Blinking non-stop, I had chronic insomnia and was probably clinically depressed. I felt an overwhelming sense of guilt over the business losses. Should I have fought harder to save them? What had I done wrong? How could I have been so careless? People must think I'm a fool.

Gradually, this period of guilt began to fade away. It was replaced with the realization that I had done my best and accomplished more than I had dreamed possible when setting out to build a career. Now it was time to accept my losses, assess what I'd learned about life – change my behaviors accordingly – and move on.

I wasn't concerned with my ability to earn a decent living. Immediately after the sale of Hume Publishing, I had accepted an offer to act as a marketing consultant for a Chicago based company. The money was good and this assignment confirmed there would be an ongoing demand for my marketing expertise. And my health was good.

Now, relieved of the all-consuming pressure involved in running a business and living a fast lane social life, I had the space, motivation, and time to begin an honest assessment of my life, both professionally and personally.

In taking a hard look at the arc of my life since founding Hume Publishing, it became clear I had been on a bullet train speeding along with no clear destination in mind. I had not taken the time to consider where this runaway train was taking me. And was it a place I wanted to arrive at?

Mulling this over during quiet evenings in the one bedroom apartment I had moved to after Penny and I separated, this realization emerged: For the past twenty years, I had been wasting vast sums of money on things I did not need, to maintain a lifestyle I did not enjoy, amongst people, many of whom I did not like or admire.

This was a shocking realization. But it was a true assessment of my life to date.

Why hadn't this sorry situation occurred to me until now? Fact is, these thoughts had crossed my mind several times, *but I ignored the signs.* There was that evening sitting alone in my beautifully furnished walnut paneled home office in our 7,000 foot home with a live-in housekeeper and cook, in one of Toronto's most luxurious neighborhoods. Penny and our daughter Amanda were out with friends. I was alone and had an awful feeling something was seriously amiss with my life. I was miserable. The money I was wasting by owning a home where most of the rooms were rarely if ever used could be better spent funding any number of worthy causes that would make the world a better place. I remember this feeling vividly, but ignored it. I often wonder if these thoughts occur to others who live in grand homes, villas, and palaces around the world.

Another warning about our excessive lifestyle occurred at a party in Palm Beach. It was hosted by a leading art dealer and attended by a platoon of newly minted billionaires, middle-east oil magnates, two members of the Kennedy clan and Ivana Trump, shortly after she'd parted ways with "The Donald". Everyone at the party was decked out as if they were heading for The Academy Awards red carpet. I tried chatting with Ivana Trump for a few minutes, but she had no interest in anything other than her own glamorous life. Within five minutes I was bored and wanted to be somewhere else. Penny was in engrossed in a discussion with one of her Toronto friends. I left the party through a rear door to the garden where I encountered a not so glamorous middle-aged woman with a pleasant face and short greyish hair. Wearing a smart business dress, rather than a high fashion designer dress, she stood out from the party crowd. She was standing alone. We began chatting and within minutes realized we has something in common. Both of us regretted coming to the party. Turned out she was the founder of a highly successful regional pizza chain which she had recently sold to a larger national company for $70,000,000. With these new found riches her husband had convinced her it might be fun living alongside the rich and famous, and had recently purchased a Palm Beach mansion. Her invitation to the party came from an art dealer who offered to help her acquire the appropriate art for her new home. He suggested an initial art budget of $2,000,000. His commission would likely be at least 25%.

She had come to the party not knowing what to expect and, within fifteen minutes, wanted to leave. This was not a place where she felt comfortable and did not understand the need for people to show off their wealth so blatantly. We spent the next hour sitting on a bench in the garden, away from the glitterati, discussing how best to live a happy life after acquiring more money than you ever dreamed possible. We both agreed it was not by buying more things you did not need. This direct, open, and intelligent woman was infinitely more interesting than Ivana Trump. I can't remember her name and never saw her again, but it's my bet she sold her Palm Beach mansion as soon as possible and headed back to her home town. I was not so smart. My life of excess carried on. It is strange, once you have climbed on to the fast-lane thrill ride it is difficult to get off, even when your instincts are sending off warning signals: this is a dangerous place to be.

As the realization that I had been living a wasteful life struck home with me, I vowed to never again acquire more than was needed to live a full and happy life. No more flashy cars, big homes, memberships in exclusive clubs, expensive jewelry, seldom visited holiday properties, or a wardrobe of high end clothes. In the future I would be a Warren Buffet kind of guy. He earns billions, lives a simple life, and is a philanthropist who gives most of his money to worthy causes. If happiness and fulfillment could be measured, it's my belief those who top the list are the Warren Buffets of the world. To be clear though, unlike Buffet, I have neither the desire nor the ability to make billions.

During this period of intense introspection much of my focus was also devoted to thinking about relationships. In assessing the people in my life it became clear to me that — after shelter, food and health — the most important factor you can control in building a happy life is the relationships you develop. This applies to those you work with, are related to, or choose to befriend. In thinking back to the happiest times in my life, both at work and socially, there was a common thread. I was not alone; the experience was always shared with someone I respected and whose company I enjoyed.

To test this theory, I listed the people with whom I had spent the most time during the last few years running the Hume Group of Companies. They fell neatly into these categories: my wife and step-daughter, work colleagues, lawyers, financiers, and consultants who provided services to The Hume Group, the rich and powerful who attended fast-lane social events including fund raisers for various charities and fancy "A list" dinner parties, members of exclusive private clubs, and with my closest friends and extended family.

Sadly, my closest friends and family had been shuffled to the bottom of the deck.

To a large extent this situation self-corrected with the fall of the Hume Group. I was simultaneously scrubbed from the contact lists of everyone but my pre Hume Publishing friends and family. Unfortunately, over the past twenty years too many of this group had either drifted away, or passed away. This included two of my closest friends, Don McGregor and Sol Bienstock who were highly influential in leading me to a happier and more fulfilling life.

Sol was the first to go, dying at the age of fifty-nine from pancreatic cancer. With his chiseled features, athletic build, salt and pepper hair, and ready smile, Sol was popular wherever he went. He was the founder and President of Bathurst Sales, Canada's largest distributor of cosmetics and beauty products. He had a heart of gold and founded "*Look Good, Feel Better*" workshops where women with cancer can learn how to manage the cancer-related impact on their appearance.

We had this in common, both of us were entrepreneurs from modest backgrounds who had built successful businesses, and we both enjoyed tennis and skiing. Sol was always at the center of the action. He and his wife Debbie had two children, Michael and Candice. We spoke every few days and got together regularly to play tennis. During the winters we sometimes went on a weeklong ski trip to Aspen or met for a day of skiing in Collingwood where Sol and Debbie owned a ski chalet.

One day, while enjoying a post tennis beer, Sol complained of a persistent high back pain and said he'd arranged a doctor's appointment to have this checked out. I called him the evening after his doctor's appointment to set up our next tennis match. Debbie answered the phone and I asked her how the doctor's appointment had gone, hoping Sol would be OK to play tennis over the weekend. She responded, "The appointment didn't go well. He is resting now, why don't you come over first thing tomorrow morning and let him tell you about the doctor's visit".

When I arrived at their place the following morning Debbie was clearing away the breakfast dishes; Sol was upstairs getting dressed. She called to let him I'd arrived and started to cry. He came into the kitchen a few minutes later. When I asked what was going on he crossed the room, gave me a huge hug, and said, "It was the worst possible news. Its pancreatic cancer and, at most, I've got another three months."

A chill coursed through my body. This couldn't be happening. When the moment had passed, Sol suggested that he, Debbie, and I walk to a nearby coffee shop to talk over the situation. It was a perfect early summer day. The trees were showing off their newly minted shiny green leaves; the sky was a brilliant blue. We walked to the coffee shop in silence, heads bowed. No one knew what to say. As we sat down at a table on the coffee shop's patio, Sol broke the spell. He said, "Well there's one positive aspect to this situation. Yesterday I was dealing with about twenty different problems. Today, I have only one."

Over cappuccinos we discussed what had to be done. Sol wasn't giving up hope and wanted to devote all of his time and energy searching for alternative treatment options.

He wanted Debbie to spend her time helping Candice and Michael deal with the situation, and familiarize herself with Sol's life insurance and investments so she would know what to do financially in the event he didn't survive. After a while I left them to sort out how best to deal with their ordeal.

Later in the day Sol called and asked me to visit him at home that evening. When I arrived it was clear he and Debbie were having a rough time. He asked if I would assist him in the search for alternative pancreatic cancer treatment options and be with him in discussions with doctors. He wanted me to take notes and ask questions that might not occur to him. Sol had already come up with a list of doctors and clinics in the US, Mexico and Canada that he intended to approach. I agreed to be there for him.

The next day, we had our first phone conversation with a US doctor and a meeting with a Toronto based pancreatic cancer specialist who agreed to visit Sol at home in the week. After the conversation with the US doc, I went home to write up notes on the conversation. Sol was going to take the family dog for a walk in the park. It was agreed I would drop by his place in the evening to review our conversation with the US doctor and look over brochures from cancer treatment clinics in the US and Mexico.

When I arrived at Sol's place that evening, he was in his home office smoking a marijuana joint and asked me to join him. A friend had suggested marijuana to help in dealing with his stress. He was excited and said he wanted to share a wonderful experience he had that afternoon. I assumed he had come up with a promising new treatment for pancreatic cancer or found a clinic specializing in its treatment. My assumption was wrong. What I learned from Sol that evening would have an important impact on the rest of my life.

Sol and I were both doers, always focusing on what we planned to do next. But that afternoon while taking the dog for walk, Sol had no business related to-do list. So, to divert his attention from the fear associated with the cancer diagnosis, he decided to focus on the experience he was participating in at that moment. All that mattered was the here and now. He consciously felt the warmth of the sun as it soaked into his shoulders, listened to the birds singing, and marveled at the beauty, vivid colors, and intricacies of the flowers in his neighbor's garden. This experience gave him a sense of peace. For almost an hour, his mind was diverted was from thinking non-stop about his cancer diagnosis. That day, Sol discovered the wonders of mindfulness. This is what he wanted to share with me.

The term "mindfulness" wasn't new to either of us but, before that evening, it was just some new-age concept we had never taken the time to explore. Sol challenged me to take a mindful walk the following day and then meet to discuss the experience. With no expectations of a cosmic breakthrough, I took my first mindful walk before breakfast the next morning. It was a half hour trek through a ravine near our home. I'd done the route hundreds of times, usually in the early morning. I had used the time to plan out details of the day ahead, and think through specific issues that needed to be addressed. But this day I blocked out all thoughts about my business day. Instead, I paid close attention to the plants and wild flowers, listened to the birds and, instead of jumping over the creek, I stopped to watch the water as it gurgled along. Never before had I realized there was watercress in the creek, or noticed its deep rich greenness. Then I saw a salamander swimming up-stream. I became so fascinated by the salamander and the discovery of watercress so close to my home that I lost track of time. A half hour had simply evaporated into thin air.

When we met that evening there was nothing new to report on the medical front. Instead, we engaged in an evening-long marijuana enhanced discussion on living a mindful life. We both regretted not being aware of this phenomenon sooner.

Although it was never discussed, as the days and weeks passed with no medical breakthrough Sol becoming increasingly weaker and seemed resigned to the fact he was dying. Having accepted this reality, he became almost obsessed with the concept of living a mindful life. He urged me to write a book on the topic. He was adamant in declaring that everyone should be aware of this life-enriching approach to living.

We continued our discussions and daily experiments with mindful living until Sol's pain management needs could no longer managed at home and he was taken to the hospital. He passed away within a week of being admitted.

Since that time I have made an effort to live a mindful life. Now I take long walks several times each week, and during these outings my attention is focused, not on personal or business issues, but on my surroundings. Even though I often follow the same path, each day's walk is always fresh and interesting. I am aware of the wind and breezes, cloud cover, wild flowers coming into bloom, those now past their prime, the changing seasonal light. I notice birds and listen to their songs. During these walks time seems to melt away and when they are over I feel refreshed and energized. Even though I have stopped the practice of trying to consciously solve problems during my walks, the solutions often pop into my head through some auto-pilot system that takes place in my brain while in a state of mindfulness. For all this, I am forever grateful to Sol.

The wisdom I picked up from Don McGregor gave me new and valuable wisdom on how to better manage important personal relationships. Don and I were close friends from the age of nine when the Humes moved into a home just around the corner from the McGregors. Don, with his ready smile and sharp wit, was always the life of the party. He was one of the few close friends I spent significant time with even when I was living life in the fast lane. Don owned a farm located about a two hour drive east of Toronto and, whenever possible, I accepted his standing invitation to spend a weekend at the farm. This was a great place to get in touch with the real world and spend time on outdoor activities — mending fences, occasionally chasing down runaway cows, or painting. When you own a farm there is always something that needs a new coat of paint. After dinner most evenings we'd sit around the kitchen table discussing life. As well, we got together regularly in the city and at the farm to play golf. This is a sport at which neither of us excelled, but we enjoyed it nonetheless. He was a true salt of the earth man. Don, Peter

Copland and I, were life-long friends, and entrepreneurs who had founded successful businesses. Don's was Permafleur, Canada's leading distributor of artificial flowers and decorative products. He and his wife Molly ran the business.

Don had one quality that sets him apart from anyone else I have known: his incredibly diverse group of close friends. Besides Peter Copland and me, his inner circle included the CEO of a large Atlanta based company, a young man who drives a cement truck, the senior partner at one of Canada's leading wealth management companies, and the owner/operator of a small dairy farm.

In his late sixties, Don was diagnosed with colon cancer and passed away within days of turning seventy. His illness was a long difficult period for both he and Molly. During much of this time Don was unable to work and Molly had to take the lead in managing their business. To help out, I was spending much of my leisure time with Don. During this period we discussed his thoughts on relationships and, for the first time, I understood how he had successfully maintained such a diverse and close inner circle of friends.

When it was clear his days on earth were winding down, Don wanted to spend what time he had left with the people he felt closest to. He was also concerned that, when news of his imminent departure leaked out, many of the people who considered him a good friend would be wanting to drop by for a visit. He didn't have the strength or energy to take these calls and asked if I would take on the role of his gatekeeper. He wanted me to reach out to his closest friends and arranged for them to have quality private time with him over the next couple of months.

He gave me a spreadsheet with his friend's names and contact information. The list was broken into his inner circle with whom he wanted to spend the most possible time, another group who I was to get in touch with and let them know he was ill, but discourage them from trying to arrange a visit. As well, he asked me to get in touch with another group after he'd gone, to give them the news.

Some of these would not be easy calls to make. But through this experience Don had taught me an important lesson about relationships. Don't take relationships for granted. Choose your friends carefully, and actively nurture those that give you the most pleasure. And avoid people who are toxic or unpleasant.

This approach to relationships is a model I try to follow.

For me, perhaps the biggest obstacle in finding the path to a better life was coming to terms with my failed marriage to Penny. Why didn't we work out as a couple? Penny has many fine qualities. She is smart, attractive, ambitious, a hard worker, a gifted speaker, and a leader who helped build and manage important non-profit organizations. She comes from a large close family. We shared common interests including theatre, art, and music. If ever I needed medical assistance, even now, Penny would come running and ensure I received the best possible care.

However, Penny revels in the role of being a superb hostess and party planner. For many years she organized major parties at The Toronto Film Festival. She loves throwing elegant dinner parties and bringing interesting people together. She is attracted to high profile people and enjoys living in a home that will accommodate large dinner parties and social gatherings. She is also stylish and enjoys wearing the latest fashions and networking, at large scale social functions.

With Penny leading the way, I gave this lifestyle a try but in the end discovered I much prefer living a more modest and quiet life. When Hume Publishing was gone, and we could no longer live the life Penny thrived on, we had no option but to separate. This was not her fault, nor was it mine. But one thing was certain. There was no way of bridging the differences that drove us apart.

With Penny and our very active social life now in the rear view mirror, I wanted to fill this gap by building new friendships with people of my choosing. After reflection, I realized that those whose company I most enjoy are creative, curious and smart. They enjoy discussing ideas and new concepts. They are not driven by the need to acquire wealth or power.

As the years have rolled on, many of my friends who fit this description have either died, retired or moved away from Toronto. This loss diminished the quality of my life. Because I've made a commitment to do whatever is necessary to make the best of every day of my life — regardless of my age — I decided to refurbish my pool of close friends. I invited a group of men whom I had met over the past few years and who seemed interesting, but I did know well to join me in forming a book club. This has been a wonderful experience for everyone in the group and created several vibrant new friendships.

Living a long and fulfilling life has many parallels to sailing a boat. You must have a clear idea of your destination, periodically assess your current position and the condition of your vessel, and continually make the necessary course corrections and boat repairs. And, as you age, you must also plan your days based on steadily diminishing physical capabilities.

I'm now in my late eighties and thoroughly enjoying life even as I get ever closer to the front of the line when my ship will reach port and the journey is over. This reality makes every day special and I intend to make the most of it.

Chapter 19

Discovering True Happiness

- - - - - - - - -

By 2006 my life was back on track and heading in the right direction, but there was one important milestone that continued to elude me. I had never found that perfect girlfriend and soul mate I'd yearned for since my teenage years. Had either Patricia or Penny been the right partner, those marriages would have been strong enough to survive both the good and the bad times we encountered during life's journey.

With this realization and a fast-shortening runway, I committed myself to an all-out effort to track down that elusive soulmate and life partner. The first step was to have clarity on the qualities we needed to share to find true happiness and fulfilment. After much thought, here is the list of qualities I wanted to share with a life partner:

- We would have compatible interests. Mine are art, music, words, theatre, some travel, and living a physically active life.
- We must share the same philosophy of life. I lean left both politically and socially and prefer to collaborate and compromise when issues arise.

- We would share equally in the day-to-day management of our life and financial affairs.
- We needed to live life at the same pace. I prefer to live life at a leisurely pace having a few close friends with shared interests.
- We would enjoy a crackling physical attraction to each other.
- My ideal partner would have a great sense of humor laced with fun and never be hurtful. Her smile would light up my day.

Having established the qualities for my ideal partner, the next step was devising a strategy to find her. At my age, there was no time to waste.

And I was not prepared to compromise in finding my soul mate. But where to begin? I am basically shy and have never developed an ability to immediately engage with women at social gatherings such as at a party or a bar. And none of my friends was reaching out to match me up with someone they knew.

Commercialized dating services did not feel right for me. However, with no other alternative, I decided to investigate further. An evening spent checking out online dating services was reassuring. There were some that catered to older people, and the women whose profiles I checked out looked interesting. Based on this research, but with serious reservations, I signed up for a one-month trial with a dating service that catered to the 50 plus market.

With the decision made to try an online dating service, I was going to proceed with caution and use the same approach to dating that had proven effective in building business relationships.

I did not want waste my time, or the time of women who were using the service. So before contacting anyone, the first step was to restrict my outreach to women whose age was plus or minus mine wittenhin 10 years. She must live a stable family focused life with no multiple divorces and live in the Toronto region. We needed to have simpatico interests and values as noted above. And anyone who looked to be living life in the fast lane would not make the cut.

The number of women matching these criteria was in the hundreds. This was narrowed down by reading every word of their online profile and the personal statements required by this dating service.

This research took weeks. Checking out interesting women, I often stayed up until close to midnight after a long day at the office. But it was important work. It had to be done to the best of my ability. Eventually the field was narrowed down to eight attractive women and one led the field by a wide margin. Her name is Barbara Brown, a widow with four grandchildren. She had one appealing attribute not on list of qualities I hoped to find in my perfect partner. She is a Brit, and I have long been a great fan of British theatre, TV, and music.

Before making a first overture to Barbara, I carefully crafted a longish email using the selling tactics picked up from working with the top-gun copywriters. The email worked like magic. She accepted an invitation to have dinner with me the following Friday.

On our first date, she let me know she likes to be called Babs. Widowed for several years, she had been using the dating site for a couple of years and was cautious when meeting a man for the first time. Babs insisted that first get togethers take place in a public setting at either a coffee shop or restaurant. She preferred academics and highly placed retired military men.

I am neither an Oxford professor nor a retired army general, but my letter of introduction struck a special chord with Babs. She agreed that I could pick her up at home. Obviously, I'd picked up some copy writing skills over the past twenty years.

When picking up Babs for our first date I was greeted by a slim elegant woman with a beautiful face and glorious warm smile framed by short blonde hair. She was wearing a simple black dress. As we crossed the street to my car she asked, in her posh English accent, "might I take your arm." This woman had class.

From the outset our conversation was warm and easy. As the evening progressed, we discovered we had more in common than was obvious from our dating site postings. We both had backgrounds in publishing, we had regularly dined at the same restaurants. I had done business with her boss at a publishing company where she had worked. While enrolled in a PhD program at McMaster University, Babs had worked with Dr. John Evans the founding Dean of McMaster University's medical school who also chaired my company's Medical advisory board. We ended up being the last couple to leave the restaurant that Friday evening. When dropping Babs off at home, I suggested we meet again for brunch on Sunday. She agreed and I headed for home floating on a cloud.

As I was to learn later, Babs too was floating on a cloud after our first date. This distracted her from fulfilling a promise made to her best friend earlier in the day. Upon learning Babs was being picked up at home by a man she had never met, her friend was apoplectic. She insisted Babs report in upon returning home safely after our date. However, Babs was so pleased with the evening she forgot to call her friend. Then, when sleeping soundly at 2:00 AM she was awakened by the ringing of her phone. It was her friend who thought it best to try reaching Babs on her mobile before calling the cops to report her missing in action.

The Sunday brunch was a continuation of our wonderful Friday evening, and that afternoon, Babs came with me to help pick out a new autumn jacket. It seemed we were meant to be together. However, as you know from reading earlier chapters in this memoir, start-ups do not always go well for me.

The next morning, I sent Babs an email letting her know how much I had enjoyed the time we had spent together over the weekend. Within an hour, she sent a terse reply saying she was unable to meet me again. It seems she had been seeing an Oxford professor who she quite liked but had thought the relationship was over. However, he had called her the previous evening and they had agreed to give it another try. I was devastated.

At that time Bab's professor friend was traveling. It would be a couple of months before he would be returning to Toronto. Learning this, I let Babs know that, although disappointed, I understood her situation. Perhaps we could stay in touch and maybe take in an occasional movie during the lonely months before her professor returned to Toronto.

In the meantime, I was back to square one in my quest for the perfect partner. There was little to choose between the next four prospects on my list and I decided to meet each of them as soon as possible. Over the next week, I dined with all four at the same French bistro. All were attractive and intelligent, but... But I was smitten by Babs and could not get her off my mind.

Two weeks after our last phone call, and after meeting with four other women, I called Babs and suggested we take in a movie, and maybe have dinner. She accepted my invitation.

During dinner before the movie, we picked up where we were two weeks ago — before I was dumped. Conversation flowed effortlessly; it was an absolute joy being with Babs. After the movie, I drove her home and parked immediately behind her brand new bright red Mini Cooper S. She was proud of that little car. Sitting there she said, "I am so glad you called, you've been much on my mind, and I'd like to see more of you. I have told David (her prof), that he is not the right man for me." With that wonderful news, I leaned over and gave her a first kiss. It was warmly received. At this point I came within a hair of destroying our budding relationship.

When dropping Babs off at the end of the evening I had expected her to say thank you for a pleasant evening and get out of the car. When the conversation took a more promising turn, I forgot to turn off the engine. With my foot on the break, it idled away during our conversation. When leaning over to give Babs a first kiss my foot slipped of the brake, the car moved forward and pranged the back of her brand new Mini. We were both stunned. A quick check indicated no damage had been done. At this point she gave me a second kiss, and we arranged to get together later in the week. From this point, our relationship blossomed and six months later we decided it was time to try living together.

This saga is being recounted in some detail as I would like to think this experience can serve as an inspiration for others on what to expect when entering a new relationship later in life.

Upon moving in together our relationship blossomed, but a few strains prevented us from the full bonding I had hoped we could achieve. We both learned, in all aspects of life, trust must be earned and it does not happen overnight. It takes time and patience, not one of my virtues. After a few months of co-habiting, we decided to rent a condo in Collingwood, a holiday community north of Toronto, so we could have time apart to work out our relationship. This did not work out quite as expected. It turned out we were calling each other several times a day even when living apart. In the end, this time apart strengthened our relationship. It shone a spotlight on our need to be with each other every day. During this period, I was riding my bike for two to three hours several times a week. For me, this was great time to think about life's opportunities and challenges.

While biking through the woods my thoughts focused on Babs. Clearly, we loved one another and, to make the relationship work, I had to be more trusting and accepting of who she is.

It seems Babs and I were on the same wavelength. Within a few months, we dropped the idea of spending time apart. Instead, we embraced all that is good in our relationship. As the months rolled on, it became clear, my quest to find the love of my life was finally over. Each day of our relationship fills me with a sense that all is right with the world.

Babs has enlightened me on what is important to live a fulfilling and happy life. She is an avid gardener and has taught me the joy that comes from caring for a garden. In my previous life, we owned a huge home with an award-winning rose garden maintained by a professional gardening service. I never gave much thought to the rose garden. It was just a space to visit occasionally.

With Babs urging, I am now playing a hands-on role in our garden. She taught me how to properly trim rose bushes and protect them from aphids and cold winters. I have learned about climbing roses, blanket roses, and shrub roses. She has taught me to appreciate the subtle colors and leaf formations of various rose genres. My favorite is New Dawn, a climbing rose. The more I learn about gardening through this mindful hands-on experience, the more pleasure it gives back. This too has made my life more fulfilling as has the awareness of being mindful in everything I do.

For the past fifteen years, Babs and I have lived in Toronto's Cabbagetown neighborhood, North America's largest existing stand of Victorian homes.

Even during the Covid 19 pandemic, when traveling and meeting with friends is not possible, we have found ways to enjoy every day. We are both music lovers. Before the pandemic, we would be out every week taking in a variety of musical events ranging from Jazz clubs to Tafelmusik baroque classical concerts. Now we get together every afternoon before dinner and listen to classic jazz accompanied by a fine single malt scotch. The artists we enjoy range across the entire spectrum of jazz from a Brea Slosberg, a brilliant young trumpet player/singer to Ella Fitzgerald and Louis Armstrong, Miles Davis, Ben Webster, Oscar Peterson, John Coltrane, B. B. King, Duke Ellington, and Dina Washington. We crank up the volume and mindfully listen to the music. This daily ceremony has taught us an important life lesson. Nothing enhances the joy of listening to music more than sharing it with someone you love. As Shakespeare instructs us, *"If music be the food of love, play on."*

Like everyone else on the planet, my life is not perfect and missteps in the past can never be erased. But now I am living with true happiness and fulfilment, and it has nothing to do with having more money, toys, or power.

And I remain an active entrepreneur. While spending time in Collingwood, I would meet regularly with Peter Lush, a good friend who owned one of the region's major real estate brokerages. He was less than pleased with the performance of the real estate agents who worked for Lush Realty. We were discussing this one evening when Peter said, "You are a marketing expert, can you come up with a strategy that will increase the productivity of my real estate agents." With time on my hands, I accepted the challenge.

Over the next couple of months, I developed an email-based marketing strategy that was tested with Peter's Realtors. It worked and their production increased dramatically. Sadly though, Peter developed cancer and died a few months later.

After Peter's death, when I was again living full time in Toronto, I decided to further develop this marketing plan for Realtors and make it available to individual real estate agents in the US and Canada under the brand name Top-Tier Leads. This late in my life, I didn't want to manage the business on a full-time basis so I recruited two men in their twenties and thirties to run the business. All went well with the product development and testing. Realtors who had used the Top-Tier Leads service gave it rave reviews. Dave and Micah, the two young men who had worked with me through the service development stage, wanted to assume responsibility for marketing Top-Tier Leads in the US and Canada. This was OK with me, if they took responsibility for raising the necessary capital and had a marketing plan I could buy into.

They failed to raise sufficient capital. Based on my analysis, the marketing plan they came up with had no chance of being successful. I reached out to Chris Jessop, one of today's top-gun mass marketers and asked if she would take on the marketing of Top-Tier Leads. After checking out the service, she agreed to take on the assignment. However, despite having no experience in direct response mass marketing, and without having raised sufficient capital, Dave and Micah would not accept my recommendation, and refused to retain Chris. At a meeting to resolve this impasse, Micah and Dave insisted they knew best how to run the business.

Even though they had raised less than half the required capital needed to fund the company, they insisted on doing the marketing their way. As predicted, their marketing plan was a colossal failure. Six months later they walked away from the business.

I contacted Christine Allsop and together we are conducting a proper marketing test for the business under a new name, Network-Growth. Assuming this test is a success, Chris would take over the business, and I would retain a royalty interest in Network-Growth.

Old serial entrepreneurs carry on regardless. I'm sure they eventually die, but not too soon.

PART 5

VALUABLE LESSONS ACQUIRED ON MY JOURNEY

Chapter 20

Happiness and fulfilment

-- -- -- -- -- -- -- -- --

As a younger man, I assumed that most people ended their days bored, lonely, maybe sedated, and putting in time waiting — with some trepidation — for the final curtain to fall. Sadly, this is the case for too many of today's seniors, but life does not have to end this way. I am now 88 years old, happy, with no major health concerns, and living one of the most fulfilling stages of my life. Much of this good fortune can be attributed to my 'genius' in choosing the right parents. Seriously though, despite the fact that we cannot choose our parents, there is much we can do to control the arc of our life. The secret is building a life on the foundation of the aptitudes you are born with and your personality traits.

Throughout life's journey, I have enjoyed periods of smooth, fast, and exciting sailing, endured extended periods in the doldrums, and survived some terrifying storms that seemed certain to sink the ship. Along the way, I picked up — usually the hard way — some useful strategies for navigating the shoals everyone encounters on this exciting journey through life.

Life Lessons for entrepreneurs and business managers

Over the course of my life, I have worked both as a paid employee and as an entrepreneur. Each of these career paths can be fulfilling. Many of the life strategies discussed here are equally applicable to both employees and entrepreneurs, and some will apply only if you are an entrepreneur.

The entrepreneurial strategies discussed here derive from both my personal experiences and from my affiliation with the University of Western Ontario's National Research Center for Management Research and Development. David Leighton, this organization's Director, invited me to participate in a study entitled Entrepreneurship: Into the 90s. This invitation came after I co-authored an article entitled *Venture Equity: Profiting from Participation.* My co-Author was Monica Belcourt a professor at York University's School of Business,

My association with a major business school provided an opportunity to test some of my theories on entrepreneurship with professors from a leading business school, and other entrepreneurs participating in the study.

As a result of this experience, I wanted to fund a chair in entrepreneurial studies at Western's Business School and had notified the University of my plan, which they graciously accepted. Sadly, I had to withdraw this offer after the market crash of 1987. This was one of my most disappointing business experiences.

Business tactics and strategies

The business tactics and strategies I describe here are not technology related despite having been developed and tested over thirty years ago. They continue to be applicable today and into the future, as long as businesses are run by humanoids rather than artificial intelligence.

1. **Choose the right career path:**
    Be sure you follow a career path in a field where you are passionate about the work you do. Do not waste your life doing work you do not enjoy. Do not compromise on this. Never get into a line of work because of your parents urging, the pay is good, or because someone offers you what seems like a great opportunity. To live a fulfilling live, you must be passionate about your work.

    If you have not yet found a career where you look forward to getting to work each day, I suggest you invest in a career counselling service.

    One of the seminal events in my own life was taking an aptitude test commissioned by Link Belt when I was in my mid-twenties. At the time, I was working as a mechanical draftsman. The job was boring, and I didn't enjoy the company of my colleagues. They were good people, but our interest were not aligned. At that point in my life, I had no clue about the range of opportunities which could be open to me. My father was a dominating force. He loved engineering and, in his view, this was the career path for me. I followed his advice and ended up wasting five years of my life.

The aptitude test was paid for by my employer, but it put me on right track to seeking a job in publishing and marketing. Since landing my first marketing/publishing job at McGraw Hill, I no longer worked to live. Now I live to work. And in my late 80s, I still look forward to getting to work each day.

2. **Test, test, test:**
One of the most valuable lessons I learned early in my business career is the importance of testing. Whether you are an employee or a business owner, situations will arise where you want to make major changes. This may be a new procedure you want to introduce, new equipment you want buy, a new product or service you want to sell, or a new advertising program you want to introduce.

When these changes turn out well, you are a hero, but when they fail, you could lose your job or your business.

You can minimize the risk of failure by running small inexpensive tests, before committing to big changes. In my view, testing before committing is an essential business strategy. No matter how bright you are, everyone makes mistakes and sometimes the results can be devastating.

Here is a hard fact to showcase the vital importance of testing.

Over 40% of all start-up companies fail because there is no viable market for the goods or services they are planning to provide. In most cases, the people who found these businesses are smart and capable, but they are not infallible. Most of these failures could have been avoided by conducting a simple and inexpensive test, before committing resources to their new business. Here is an example of how to test the demand for a new product or service.

- Determine the scope of the demand by researching the number of prospective clients in the market being served. With today's online search capabilities this is usually easy to do. When the scope of the market is determined, the business founder must consider what market share they can reasonably expect to capture, or take way from competitors.
- Prepare a list of competitors operating in the target market, and compare them in terms of price, offer, and sales features. If possible gather intelligence on each competitor's sales volume.
- Assemble a database of prospective clients and their contact information. Do not include people who know the founding entrepreneur.

- Prepare a detailed description of the product or service. This will include a brief overview, a list of the features and benefits, and the price or fees that will be charged. Have this description edited or re-written by a professional copy writer or someone with experience in writing sales literature.
- Conduct a survey of prospective clients using email, direct mail, or by phone. Include an introduction stating why the survey is being conducted along with the product or service description. The survey will have three questions:

  1: Would you definitely buy this?
  2: Would you definitely not buy this?
  3: Would you consider buying this?

These surveys can be done online through a free service such as "SurveyMonkey".

The cost to conduct the research described above will likely range from $2,500 - $4,000 and will take 60 to 90 days to complete.

This is a small cost in terms of time and money compared to the ruinous losses in money, time, reputation, and the embarrassment involved in a business failure.

Before moving ahead with that multi-million dollar business idea, first conduct a test to see how prospective customers respond to your great idea. By doing this, all you have to lose is deferring your plan to get rich for a couple of months.

If the test confirms the viability of your business concept, it will be easier to recruit the people and raise the capital you will need to turn your dream to a reality.

Failing to test a new business concept was one of my most costly mistakes.

Because I had family members and friends who suffered from depression, I was convinced the world needed a patient education program to help those suffering from this debilitating condition. In response to this unmet need, I founded a new company to provide the service.

For guidance on how to package the medical service we planned to develop, I reached out to Dr. Paul Garfinkel, the Chief of Staff at Ontario's Center for Mental Health and Addiction. He was supportive of the need, and agreed to act as Chairman of an Advisory Board. With his support, we invested in developing a depression management program that received critical acclaim within the medical community.

After convincing myself this patient education program would serve an unmet need, I bypassed the step of carrying market research on the perceived need. This was a fatal oversight. When the service was launched, those who were in a depressed state did not have the motivation to enrol in the program. And, when these same patients had come through a depressed state, they simply wanted to enjoy life free of depression and were not interested in enrolling in a program that reminded them of the pain inflicted by this devastating disorder.

This was the most disappointing failure of my business career as the money raised to develop the program came from close friends and family. This disaster could have been avoided by spending a few thousand dollars on market research with sufferers of depression before developing the program.

Test your advertising messages on a regular basis. Every politician and direct sales professional knows this to be true. Get the sound bites right, and it is much easier to close the sale. This fact applies to every business. Whether you are running a software company or a restaurant, it pays to regularly test the headlines and key messaging used to market a company's services. At one point in my career, we got a 240% increase in sales by simply testing a new headline on an advertisement.

3. **Look first to strategic investors when financing a new company:**
    This strategy is only applicable to entrepreneurs. At some point most entrepreneurs require outside capital to get their business up and running or

to make a major expansion of the business. The first and most obvious sources to approach for funding are banks, angel investors, or venture capital companies.

An often overlooked source of capital is strategic investors. A strategic investor is someone who stands to gain if your company succeeds. For example, when funding was required for HUmed, we approached the owners of privately owned commercial printing companies. They were offered a deal where, if the printing company owner made an equity investment in HUmed, his/her printing company would get all of the company's printing business, as long as the required specifications were met, and prices were within 2% of prices quoted from other qualified printers.

Most of the printing company owners we approached were interested. If HUmed succeeded, they won two ways: their printing business had a major new long-term client, and the business owner had the opportunity to make a significant personal capital gain. This strategy enabled us to raise the required funding in weeks, without going through the extensive due diligence protocols required by a bank or venture capital company.

It is usually easier to negotiate better terms with a strategic supplier, because they stand to gain in two ways. My only regret is not coming up with this funding strategy when I was first raising capital for Hume Publishing.

4. **Schedule time to think and strategize:** A recent study by *The Harvard Business Review* states that senior executives spend their work time as follows: 61% on face-to-face interactions, 15% on the phone or reading, and 24% on electronic media.

Based on my experience, there is a serious omission in this time allocation. Every week, busy entrepreneurs and executives pick up an avalanche of new information. It comes through reports that cross their desk, from one-on-one conversations with colleagues and employees, through group meetings, articles in newspapers and magazines, meeting people at seminars or trade events, etc. This information cannot be absorbed, put in perspective, and analysed on the fly.

I strongly recommend that entrepreneurs and senior business executives, schedule a weekly half-day meeting with themselves. This is a time to absorb, analyse, and think about all the information they have been exposed to over the past week, and consider its impact on their business.

During this pre-scheduled time, serious uninterrupted thought can be devoted to identifying potential problems and opportunities that could be on the horizon and how to deal with problems before they get out of control.

After being introduced to the practice of booking in thinking time for myself, I adhered to this practice religiously over my career, with great success.

5. **Arrange team meetings to solve major problems and capitalize on new opportunities:** To illustrate the value of team meetings, here is a real life case study. This occurred when we decided to automate Hume Publishing's mass marketing system. To make this happen we needed outside expertise. This included an industry authority on direct-to-consumer mass marketing, and a software development engineer.

For guidance in developing an automated mass marketing system, I reached out to Bill Baker who was Vice-President Operations and Information Services at Nelson Publishing, and Alan Booth who was a Vice-President at Wunderman Direct, our ad agency. Both Bill and Alan were invited to join our core management team for a weekend think tank at a lakeside resort in Muskoka.

The development of the mass marketing system was vitally important to the company's success. We decided the most effective way to get the project underway was to arrange a weekend meeting at a location where our unified thought processes could be focused on the issue at hand, without being distracted by day-to-day work activates.

Before the meeting, all attendees received a description of the system we were planning to develop. I acted as the meeting coordinator to keep the discussion on track and we went to work.

Within an hour of starting the meeting, we ran into a serious problem. Our CFO and Marketing Manager were poles apart on the information to be gathered through the system, how it would be presented, and how often the reports would be issued. By our lunch break these differences were unresolved, and we were all on edge. If nothing else, at least we had clarity and on the issues that need to be resolved.

At this point our CFO and VP Marketing took a walk through the woods with Bill Baker, our software expert, to discuss the situation. They returned from their walk in the woods ten minutes late, grinning from ear to ear. While discussing the morning's conversation, each had picked up a clearer understanding of both the marketing and financial accounting issues involved. With this heightened clarity they were able to work out a system that met both the company's accounting and marketing needs — and more.

With the impasse between marketing and finance resolved, the balance of the meeting went smoothly. By the time it wrapped up, we knew exactly how to build our ground breaking mass marketing software, and what it would cost.

This was not the only positive development that occurred over the weekend. While driving back to Toronto with Bill Baker, I learned he was not happy in his current position at Nelson. Without this knowledge, I would never have offered him a management role with Hume Publishing.

This case study illustrates the value of team meetings in an environment where there are no day-to-day business distractions, and participants have the time and space to reach consensus on important issues.

This single meeting resulted in solutions that changed the trajectory of Hume Publishing's growth and profitability.

6. **Go to top-guns when you want something important done:**

To build the Hume Publishing business, we reached out to recruit the world's best direct response copy writers, instead of settling for second tier writers who worked on a salary for our ad agency. Although fees charged by top-gun copy writers were more than double what we had been paying to have copy written by our ad agency, the response rates to ads created by the top-guns increased response rates by over 20%! As a result, our sales and profits grew exponentially.

In most cases, there is a big payoff for getting top talent.

7. **Do not be afraid to take chances:** No matter how great the odds, as long as you believe in the cause, and no big risk is involved in failing, go for it. During my business career, I have heard many good ideas that were never pursued because of a fear of failure. Yes, failure can sometimes be painful, but you can get over it. But when you make the effort and your project works out, the satisfaction and your sense of achievement lasts forever.

When you have done the research and decided do take that big business risk, go all out and reach for the stars. The world depends on entrepreneurs to develop new and better products and services, create jobs, and make life better for everyone on the planet. Whether you are planning to open a hot dog stand or resolve the climate change crisis, aim high.

This is a principle I have lived by throughout my career. When I got my chance to be a book publisher, I wanted to publish best sellers. When I announced this to the Executive Team at McGraw Hill, they scoffed and told me not to over-reach. But I held true to my dream, and managed to publish a New York Times #1 best seller. Later, when I founded Hume Publishing, it was my goal to develop the world's best-selling home-study program. There are no statistics to verify if this goal was achieved, but over 5,000,000 individuals enrolled in my *Successful Investing and Money Management* course. When I decided to set up a family of mutual funds and market them directly to consumers, the financial pundits and industry insiders said it could not be done. But we did it, selling Hume Funds directly to over 40,000 unit holders in less than two years.

My goal now is to get this memoir on a business book best-seller list. Although this may seem like a pipe dream for a first time author nearing ninety years of age, I am setting up a marketing strategy with that goal in mind.

So, when you dream, it is my advice you aim high. You will not always achieve the big win, but if you do not try one thing is certain ... your dream has no chance of being realized. And when you do try and succeed, it is a great thrill.

8. **Develop a sounding board of highly intelligent people:** As an entrepreneur who is building a business from scratch it is a certainty that you will face challenges along the way. When these situations arise, it is helpful to have access to a

few experienced advisors with whom you can talk through issues and determine how best to move forward. In an established company, you can usually find someone within the organization to offer decision-making guidance. But with a start-up you will likely need to reach outside for the guidance you need.

9. **Just get it done:** This is my final piece of advice to budding entrepreneurs, business managers, and the self-employed. When you have to deal with something unpleasant or challenging, do not procrastinate, just get it done. From time to time you will make the wrong decision, but in the long run, it is less damaging to make an occasional mistake than losses that occur through needless procrastination.

    I believe you can only live a truly happy and fulfilling life when you have developed clear cut "principles to live by" in both your business and personal life. Let me now turn to share with you the five non-business Life Lessons that have shaped my life.

Life Lessons

1. **Do not accumulate material things you do not need:** Excess in anything is a drag in the quest for happiness and fulfillment.

When life goes well and you accumulate wealth beyond your personal needs do not hoard it in some off shore tax haven to avoid paying taxes. Instead, become a philanthropist and seek out causes where you can help those who, through no fault of these own, need help. You can make a difference.

2. **Do not hold grudges or waste your time reliving past unpleasantness and grievances:** I have seen lives — including my own — spiral out of control because of wasting time, focus, and personal resources, on things that went wrong. When consumed with negative feelings, you become miserable, non-productive and not good company for your family, friends, and colleagues. Do not get mired in situations where there is no positive way forward. It is best to recognize these situations and move on. Look for the unlimited good and positive things life has to offer. And be productive! At the end of the day we are what we do. That will be your legacy.

3. **Treasure and cultivate close personal relationships:** Expensive toys, jewelry, and grand homes will not bring happiness if you have no one to share them with. No matter how successful you become, put in the time and make the effort to cultivate and nurture fulfilling relationships. One of life's greatest pleasures is sharing good times, laughs, and truly engaging with people whose

company you enjoy. This realization hit home when I met an auto-parts billionaire who owned a 300 foot yacht he kept moored at the Palm Beach Yacht Club. Although super rich, the guy was so lonely he spent the week between Christmas and New Year alone on his shiny new toy, and was so starved for company, he would invite strangers to come on board for a tour. Although super rich, he was a sad and lonely man.

4. **By mindful in everything you do:** When building a business or career it requires discipline to slow down and enjoy the world around you and the people with whom you share life. When you go a walk, bike ride, or meet a neighbor on the street, do not focus exclusively on business related issues and problems. Give your full attention to life in the moment. Mindfully enjoy music, art, poetry, theatre, flowers, bird songs, the sun on your shoulders, the breeze rustling your hair, or the conversation. There is much beauty in this world. To get your share of it you must be mindful. Many of your unresolved issues will magically be resolved during the time you have been mindfully enjoying the world you live in.

5. **Make trust a cornerstone of your life:** Be careful who you trust and do not do business with people when you learn they have been less than trustworthy in a personal or business situation.

This I learned the hard way. And never forget, there are two sides to this coin.

6. **Do not rest on your laurels:** Do what you can to contribute to the world you live in, every day until you have nothing more to give.

The end for now. But who knows, maybe the best is yet to come.